5k and 10k
from start
to finish

5k and 10k
from start to finish

Graeme Hilditch

A & C Black • London

Published by A&C Black Publishers Ltd
36 Soho Square, London W1D 3QY
www.acblack.com

ISBN 978 14081 2728 5

A CIP catalogue record for this book is available from the British Library.

Acknowledgements
Cover photograph © Brooks Sports Inc. and Cancer Research UK
Inside photographs p x, xiii, xiv, 4, 36, 122, 124, 126–128, 143,146, 148, 152 © Cancer Research UK; p ix, 19, 62–72, 77–86, 118 © Tom Croft; p 23 © Kathryn Catto; p 149 © adidas Women's 5k Challenge event; p 151 © Great Run 2010; p 5, 8, 10, 14–15, 18,28, 30, 32–34, 39 41, 44, 55, 59–61, 74, 76, 102, 112, 114–117, 119,120 (top), 121, 130, 133, 141 © Brooks Sports Inc; p 3, 24, 87–89, 92–94, 97–100, 103–105, 107–110, 125, 137, 140, 142, 144–145, 154 © shutterstock
Illustrations by Tom Croft
Designed by James Watson
Commissioned by Charlotte Croft
Edited by Kate Wanwimolruk

The publisher would like to thank Le Spa, Cirencester for the use of the gym.

*A minimum donation of 15p from every book sold will be paid to Cancer Research UK Trading Limited, which gives its taxable profits to Cancer Research UK.

This book is produced using paper that is made from wood grown in managed, sustainable forests. It is natural, renewable and recyclable. The logging and manufacturing processes conform to the environmental regulations of the country of origin.

Typeset in 10/14pt DIN Regular by Saxon Graphics Ltd, Derby

Printed and bound in China by RR Donnelley South China Printing Co.

contents

foreword

Taking part in a 5k or 10k event is a great way to stay in shape and keep active. Living a healthy lifestyle has many benefits including helping reduce your cancer risk.

In this book, Graeme Hilditch has prepared easy-to-follow training plans tailored for both beginners and experienced runners, so even people who are not regular runners can step up to the challenge of their first 5k or 10k event and veterans can improve on their previous efforts.

Cancer Research UK offers a number of running (or jogging!) events which provide the perfect motivating goal plus the chance to do something positive and inspirational to help beat cancer. In the last 40 years survival rates have doubled and our work has been at the heart of that progress. We are fighting cancer on all fronts, finding new ways to prevent, diagnose and treat it to save more lives.

If you would like to get involved in any of our events and help us beat cancer, please visit our website www. cancerresearchuk.org

Best of luck with your training, we look forward to presenting you with your medal on the finish line!

The Race for Life team

in aid of*
CANCER RESEARCH UK
Race for Life

acknowledgements

With so many people to thank who have helped me through the highs and lows of writing this book, I am sadly not able to mention everyone.

Thank you to my parents, Lynn and Cliff, who have always been there to listen to my woes throughout the writing process and who always find time to offer their support.

Thank you to all my clients, who have – in one way or another – helped to give me an insight into the range of anxieties that can come with training for a running event.

Thank you to my forever patient wife Joanne, who not only spent a family holiday in Dubai reading through the manuscript to check for errors and general bad writing, but also tolerated an occasional grumpy and moody writer who had his fair share of bad days during the writing process.

Finally, thank you to my beautiful daughter Poppy, whose smile after a difficult day of writing never failed to lift my spirits and make me realise the important things in life.

introduction

Running is one of the most primeval and natural forms of human movement, and with its endless health benefits it's easy to see why, every year, thousands of everyday people, far from classing themselves as athletes, take up recreational running. Whether it's jogging around the local park with the dog or pounding the streets around town, running is growing in popularity as one of the most enjoyable and cheapest ways to stay in shape, make new friends and even help keep the waistline under better control.

As the popularity of running continues to soar, so does the number of 5k and 10k running events organised every year. Mass-participation charity events such as Race for Life have attracted hundreds of thousands of people from all walks of life to raise valuable funds for charity, while at the same time helping people keep their stress levels and blood pressure under control through the countless health benefits of running.

Credit crunch or no credit crunch, it seems the gloomy economic climate has served only to inspire people to slip on their running shoes and take part in one of the hundreds of 5k or 10k running events organised throughout the UK, or just take a fun gym challenge to run the distance on a treadmill.

Every year in the UK alone, over a million people take up the challenge of competing in a 5k or 10k running event, all with different reasons for taking part. Whether it's breaking the elusive 30-minute barrier for 5k or the 60-minute milestone for 10k, these challenging goals are all fantastic to aim for. But not everyone should feel pressured to push themselves to the limit of physical exertion. Although the challenge of running in these events is perhaps the thing people enjoy the most, others may decide that walking the distance is more suitable to their age, body shape or fitness level – and why not?

Without wishing to use one of the top ten clichés at the very start of the book, it's the taking part in these events that is by far the most important thing! Provided you enjoy the experience, you should never feel pressured to run if you do not feel you are capable of it.

Whether you anticipate walking, power walking, jogging or running a 5k or 10k event, this book has been written especially to help you with all aspects of your training, from what to wear on your feet, via how to stretch properly before and after a run, to what to eat and how to treat niggling injuries without spending hundreds of pounds at a physiotherapy clinic.

Although you might not be training for the illustrious marathon distance of 26.2 miles, there are still dozens of easily avoidable mistakes you might make during your training that could result in injury or lack of fitness and end up ruining your chances of enjoying taking part in your chosen event. The importance of training for a 5k and 10k event is often overlooked by many people, who think they can go it alone with little or no preparation, but thanks to my 14 years of experience as a personal trainer I know that these are often the very people who end up either injured or, worse, taken ill during the race due to, for example, poor nutrition before and/or during the event.

5k and 10k: From Start to Finish will tell you how you can fit training in around all the other things in your life – be it bridge on a Friday night or a pint with your mates while watching the football on a Saturday. You will find that not only can training be fun but your life needn't stand still while you find the time to put the kilometres into those legs – and that you can even enjoy the occasional glass of Pinot Grigio and a hearty curry with all the trimmings. What's more, you never know – the calories you burn through your training might just reshape your bum nicely, so that you can fit into those old jeans at the back of the wardrobe.

Good luck with your training and, whatever your aspirations, enjoy yourself!

1 first things first

Before you hit the streets, gym or local park and embark on your first training run, there are one or two things you need to sort out first.

First and foremost, now that you are all but committed to entering a race – don't panic or, worst of all, back out. In the early stages of training, the road ahead can seem like a never-ending one, and the prospect of jogging or running a distance you never dreamed possible can be pretty daunting.

Whether you have only just recently won your place in the race and are unsure whether you have enough time to train, or you are still wondering whether you are physically up to the challenge, please don't worry and think you are alone in having

Committing yourself

The best way to commit yourself to the race and make it difficult, in a moment of weakness, to back out, is to call as many friends and family as you can and tell them that you are entering a race and that sooner or later you'll be nagging them for sponsorship money. Not only will this prepare them to dust off their chequebooks but it makes backing out so much harder – you'll have to enter now if only to save face!

these feelings of anxiety. A little apprehension before you've even taken your first training step are so normal they are almost a given – especially if you are a 5k or 10k virgin.

what to expect

Training and preparing for a running event is a fantastic experience, and the journey from struggling to be able to run for a bus to being able to finish a 5k or 10k course is far more rewarding than you could ever imagine.

Provided you train properly and get your preparations off on the right foot (then the left ... etc.) the coming weeks of training will give you a real focus and perhaps even something to really look forward to. If you're a newcomer to the world of jogging, the notion that for the next few months you'll actually look forward to getting hot and sweaty three or four times a week might seem crazy, but if you look at how many people run 5k and 10k events in a year there must be something in it. They can't all be mad!

Although it can take a few weeks to adapt to a new routine, which invariably involves heading out for a jog instead of putting your feet up with a glass of wine watching *Eastenders*, I can guarantee you'll enjoy the 10–12 weeks of training so much that you'll be itching to sign up for another 5k or 10k event.

But let's not get carried away just yet ...

⁝pre-training checklist

Wherever you rank yourself on the scale of athleticism, before you begin preparing your body to tolerate the demands of running (or power walking) training, it is a good idea to sit down and go through the following checklist before you take your first step.

Even if you have been exercising on and off for the past few months and feel you could easily take on a 5k or 10k right now in your slippers, there are still a few things you should consider before undertaking any one of the training schedules included in Chapter 5.

All too often, runners dive into their training regime all guns blazing without thinking about one or two little additions that could make their training far less susceptible to annoying injuries, make it a lot safer and, above all, a lot more fun.

Here are some of the questions you need to ask yourself before you hit the road:

- Has your heart had an 'MOT' recently? Do you need a check-up?

- What are your race ambitions?

- Are you going it alone or training with friends?

- Do you have any joint niggles that could cause discomfort during training?

- How much time can you dedicate to training?

- Are your running shoes up to the job?

Are you roadworthy? Get a heart MOT

It doesn't matter if you're a 25-year-old whippersnapper or a mature grandparent of 75, if you are in any doubt about whether your heart, lungs or limbs are up to the challenge of training for a running event, it's a good idea to visit your GP and have an 'MOT', to check that you're roadworthy. If it's been a few years since you've participated in any form of intense exercise such as jogging, or if you're carrying a little bit more weight than you'd like, a 10-minute consultation with your doctor will give both of you an insight into the condition of your cardiovascular health and reveal if there are any underlying problems that could be exacerbated by training. As rare as this might be, it's best to be on the safe side.

Bad boys

Without wishing to stereotype people (but of course I'm about to do just that), through my experience as a personal trainer, I have found that men are by far the worst at admitting that they might benefit from a medical check-up before starting an exercise regime. I've lost count of the number of times potential male clients have laughed off my recommendation that they visit their GP, with lines like 'Oh, I'm fine. There's nothing wrong with my blood pressure' or 'I'm still fit; I played rugby at university'.

These immortal phrases more often than not result in blood pressure readings in excess of 160/100 (120/80 is normal) and cholesterol levels way higher than they should be, leaving me biting my lip to avoid the immortal phrase 'I told you so' slipping out.

If any of this sounds familiar, yet the thought of making an appointment with your GP still seems a

little tedious and probably unnecessary, why not take this opportunity to schedule a 'Wellman' appointment? These comprehensive check-ups are undertaken by your GP at the surgery and give you a thorough medical MOT and the peace of mind that 'everything', not just your heart and lungs, is still in good working order.

What to expect

Unless you have a history of poor cardiovascular health or have had recent surgery, your GP is not likely to perform any invasive tests on you, but will simply ask what you anticipate your training schedule will be and – worst case scenario – check the following three things:

1 Body mass index (classifies your body composition with a calculation based on your weight and height to determine if you are under or overweight)

2 Blood pressure

3 Heart rate

Although many people feel they are being over cautious if they book an appointment to see their GP before training, it is an absolute necessity if you have been previously diagnosed with any heart condition or you are on medication.

As innocent as little white pills may look, certain medications such as beta-blockers have a direct influence on how fast your heart beats, so advice from your GP on how to train for an event is vital. He or she may very well give you the all clear, but suggest that you train with a heart rate monitor (see chapter 4) so that you know how hard your heart is working during your training sessions.

Provided your GP is happy with the condition of your cardiovascular system and has given you personalised advice on other health conditions you may have, such as asthma, arthritis or even pregnancy, there is no reason why, health-wise, you aren't good to go and ready to start your training regime.

Is it really necessary?

Although the need for a physical going-over by your doctor may seem a little over the top, every year previously undetected health conditions have been diagnosed at exactly this stage of training preparation and have saved countless lives.

All this might sound alarming and you may now be wondering what on earth you've let yourself in for, but rest assured that any form of physical exercise, from walking to running, is incredibly safe and, in the long term, one of the best ways to ward off heart disease, reduce stress levels and improve your overall health. While it's important to be aware of some of the health conditions that newcomers to jogging should be aware of, provided you have had a

Expert corner

According to the Blood Pressure Association, one in three adults in the UK (that's 16 million people) has high blood pressure, yet one third of them are totally unaware as there are no obvious symptoms. If you get only one thing checked out before you begin training, make sure it's your blood pressure.

check up with your GP to screen for any underlying health problems, you can be confident that you can embark on your training regime without fear of suffering any ill effects on your very first run.

Age is just a number

If you class yourself as more of a mature runner and you are taking part in an event to help you stay in shape and remain active, you will certainly not be alone – 5k and 10k events have become hugely popular with older competitors, and why not? Whether you're 50, 60 or knocking on the door of 70, there is nothing to stop you taking part in an event, provided you have a check-up with your GP first, and follow all the guidelines outlined in the training plans in Chapter 6.

The physical benefits of exercise have been well documented for years, and growing scientific evidence is revealing how effective regular activity is at improving our mental health, too. According to the Chief Medical Officer, regular aerobic exercise – such as power walking or jogging – helps to improve cognitive performance in older age, especially in tasks that make demands on our attention, such as general concentration and problem solving.

So, if the golden years of your twenties, thirties and forties are behind you, and you are flirting with

Expert corner

According to the National Coalition for Active Ageing, 81 per cent of men and 87 per cent of women over the age of 55 do not achieve the recommended levels of physical activity. This should give wavering entrants no better incentive to sign up for a nearby 5k or 10k event. Regular training will not only give you a real goal to aim for but will help to ward off countless diseases commonly contracted in our latter years.

Performing moderately intense physical activity (such as power walking or jogging) has been shown to reduce the risk of heart disease, obesity, high blood pressure, diabetes and even some cancers.

Above all, remember the old adage, 'Jogging might not necessarily add years to one's life, but it certainly adds life to one's years'.

the idea of taking part in an event, there's every reason to take the plunge and go for it. You might not be the first to cross the line (and it may even surprise you that you may not be the last!), but jogging a 5k or 10k event is great fun and, you never know, you might be tempted to do it all again.

What are your race ambitions?

Before you take your very first step out of the front door all kitted out and ready to go, it is a good idea to first decide what your goal is for the upcoming 5k or 10k event, as this will have a major influence on the way you approach the weeks of training ahead.

If, like so many aspiring joggers, you have a full-time job, a family to look after and barely enough time to brush your teeth let alone put some kilometres into your legs for training, you've got to be realistic about the amount of time you're going to be able to put aside every week to train.

You might find it easy in the early stages of training – your enthusiasm will be at its peak to set everything aside, including work and family, to find the time to fit in training runs but often, as missed jobs and commitments catch up with you, training regularity inevitably decreases. It's all too easy for that goal of breaking 30 minutes for 5k or 60 minutes for 10k to fade away and become a distant dream. You suddenly realise that you have bitten off more than you can chew.

If you are the competitive type and really want to get round the course as quickly as you can, whether it's by running or power walking, I'd be tempted to be a little conservative with your race ambitions to start with, to save disappointment and avoid putting undue pressure on yourself. That way, you'll be satisfied if you reach your revised (more realistic) goal, and even more chuffed if you manage to get close to your initial target.

A tip for the nervy novice

If you have just signed up for your first ever event and are happy to condition your body to just get round the course in one piece, enjoy yourself and simply soak up the carnival atmosphere, then your main focus for training is to enjoy it and not put any pressure on yourself.

Many people who train to finish in a specific time or to beat a friend tend to sacrifice the enjoyment of the event for achieving a fast time, which can take the edge off what is supposed to be a bit of fun and a good way to stay in shape and lose a few pounds.

Walk, jog or run, if the time it takes you to finish the race is the least of your concerns, then the focus of your training regime should be to exercise regularly and gradually increase your training distance every week or so, without any emphasis put on how fast you run. Run for enjoyment, or, as the slogan for leading shoe manufacturer Brooks says, 'just Run Happy!'

So, strap on that MP3 player, listen to some funky tunes and enjoy the fact that every training walk/run you complete is burning calories, improving your health but, above all, conditioning your heart and lungs to tolerate the rigours of the 5k/10k event you have entered.

Find a training partner

Training with a friend or three is a fantastic way to stay motivated, and if you enjoy group activities it can make the upcoming weeks of training far more fun – especially when it's blowing a gale and the prospect of facing a long run all on your own is far from appealing.

Unlike a marathon, the beauty of 5k and 10k events is that, no matter how unfit you are, the distance is well within the means of most people, so coercing a friend to enter the event with you is fairly easy. Of course, for some very reluctant friends, bribery or emotional blackmail may be the answer! But, more often than not, it's possible to find two or three like-minded work colleagues or friends to train with you

'To help make training more fun, I found that signing up to an event with a group of friends helped keep me motivated.'

'Always try and start your training on the flat – even the smallest of hills can seem like mountains when you first start out!'

Caroline Ferguson and Lydia Eden

– and to share the experience with you on the day of the race.

Sharing the burden of training, the occasional muscle twinge and of course the excuse for a few private evenings away from partners to discuss 'race tactics' over a glass of wine can be really uplifting and part of your weekly social calendar. So, if you have any friends in mind who you think you might be able to persuade to join you, give them a call, tell them to buy this book and don't take no for an answer!

Training with pre-existing injuries

One of the most frustrating problems facing prospective runners is starting their training with a pre-existing knee/hip/ankle/back injury, which they fear will only be made worse when they begin their training regime.

An old sports injury picked up back in college days, or an unexplained knee problem that comes and goes for no apparent reason, are infuriating and often cause people to quit training before it's even really started, or force people who desperately want to run the event to be resigned to walking it instead.

If you are one of the many hopeful race participants who has a joint pain that nags at you every time you head out for even a short jog or run, you have to decide now what you want to do about it.

Put simply, you have three options.

1 Discuss the problem with your GP during your check-up; she or he may choose to refer you to a physiotherapist.

2 Seek specific professional help from an osteopath, physiotherapist or other recommended practitioner.

3 Enter the race with the mindset of walking, but follow the exercises outlined in Chapter 7, which addresses common causes of joint pain.

Don't despair

There are so many different reasons for painful joints but thankfully an equal number of ways to alleviate the pain and get you running without discomfort, such as stretching and strengthening exercises, as well as massage. Try not to get too despondent – all hope of taking part in your chosen event is certainly not lost.

The sands of time

If you're lucky enough to have passed the doctor's medical with flying colours, have a clear idea of how fast you want to run the race, are free from annoying joint niggles, and have managed to shamelessly bribe a friend or two to run with you, the next big challenge is finding the time to dedicate to training.

How to find the time to train

- If you have kids and you're lucky enough to live near your extended family, take the opportunity to give them 'grandparent bonding time' on a Saturday or Sunday afternoon. That way, you can fit in a training run and maybe a relaxing and peaceful cup of coffee afterwards, on your own or with your training partner.

- If you are training with a friend, why not play the 'We're doing this run for charity' card to your partners and let them take the kids for a an hour or two once a week, while you squeeze in a training run – and of course a post-run coffee.

- Not always the most popular option, but setting the alarm 45 minutes earlier just once a week to fit in an early-morning run is the perfect way to tick off a training session. Morning runs are invigorating and, although it might be hard pulling back the duvet as dawn is breaking, you'll feel great for the rest of day.

- Fitting in a lunchtime jog while at work is not always easy due to lack of showering facilities, but if you can squeeze in 30 minutes in your lunch break, just once a week, it's the perfect chance to get some kilometres into your legs. Even if you can only manage a power walk up a hill, it's better than nothing – and it all adds up.

- Emotionally blackmailing your boss might not be conventional work practice, and on most people's list of 'things to do today', but asking him/her if you can come into work an hour earlier in the morning, so you can leave an hour earlier in the afternoon to fit in a run (for your 5/10k charity event) is a request that they are likely to find difficult to refuse.

For those who are not used to exercising on a regular basis, integrating a jogging programme into your already hectic lifestyle can seem like an impossible task, but with a little help from friends and family, and a small restructuring of your weekly routine, you'll be amazed that in actual fact the time is there – you've just got to look for it.

Of course, everyone reading this book will have different professional and personal commitments to work and family, but by taking note of the tips to the left you should be able to find a gap or two in the diary to fit in some decent training sessions. It's not always easy but, trust me, it is possible.

To say that it's easy to find the time to train would be incredibly dishonest, as it can be really tricky in world where we could all do with an eight-day week, but by juggling a few things around and directing a charm offensive at certain people, there is always a way to find time to train.

2

dress to impress

If you have ever taken part in, or just witnessed, a big 5k or 10k running event, the one thing you will certainly have noticed is the diverse range of running attire people choose to wear during the race. From waves of pink cowboy hats to women (and men) wearing nothing on their torso but a brightly coloured brassiere, it won't surprise you to hear that the dress code at virtually all events is fairly lax, and pretty much anything goes. As long as you don't break any public decency laws, there's nothing stopping you from wearing whatever takes your fancy.

Whatever you anticipate wearing on the day of the race, training in unconventional running kit is generally not advised. Your skin and the other moving parts might be able to handle 90 minutes or so of jogging on race day, but 10 weeks plus of preparation in unsupportive bras, loose boxers and

Why sports bras are best

Those tired old jokes about the need for 'over-the-shoulder boulder holders' for generously endowed women may well be rife, particularly when it comes to running, but the importance of wearing a good-quality and well-fitted running bra, no matter what your size, must not be underestimated. According to a survey by a leading sports bra manufacturer Shock Absorber, a staggering 68 per cent of women do not wear a sports bra during exercise, a statistic that must be addressed in order to preserve the long-term health of breast tissue.

Shock Absorber commissioned research from the University of Portsmouth and teamed up with Dr Joanna Scurr, a leading breast health expert. They found that, while running, breasts move in a continuous 'figure of eight' pattern, which can lead to rubbing or chafing as a result of the repetitive motion. In addition, repeating this motion for long periods of time gradually stretches the Cooper's ligaments, which are ultimately responsible for supporting breast tissue. Once these ligaments have been stretched, there is no going back and the resulting breast sag is irreversible.

Sports bras are designed to significantly reduce breast movement during physical exercise, and help to protect your breasts from both breast pain and stretched ligaments. So, ladies, for the long-term health of your breasts, it's a really good idea to invest in a high-quality sports bra; they might not be cheap but they are certainly worth it.

ill-fitting tops is not only uncomfortable during a jog but also bad for you in the long run, especially for women.

∴coming out of the clothing closet

If you have been 'inactive' for a few years, there's every chance that in preparation for your first training run, you'll be digging around the back of your wardrobe to find an old pair of tracksuit bottoms, a well-worn Rolling Stones T-shirt and a scuffed pair of Green Flash trainers.

As well as they may have served you back in your school or college days, now is a good time to hit the high street before you hit the road, and kit yourself out with some good-quality jogging clothes and trainers. They needn't cost the earth, but wearing appropriate running gear throughout your training will save you from a range of nuisances – from chafing to sore knees. Plus, there is something special and almost empowering about heading out for a jog in good-quality, good-looking running kit. In the same way that you feel important and empowered when you slip on a new Armani suit (I wish!), heading out for a run in swanky running kit can actually help you enjoy the experience so much more. It might not make you run faster but at least you'll look and feel great.

Of all the kit you can buy, by far the most important (and pricey) item you need is a good-quality pair of running shoes. Your old trainers or squash shoes might feel comfortable now, but after 45 minutes of walking or running on the roads, comfortable will be the last word on your mind.

∴kit essentials

Running shoes

Ask any running expert and they will tell you that finding the right pair of running shoes is vital to help you with your race preparations and help avoid injury though there are runners out there who beg to differ.

In recent years, there has been an alarming increase in the number of hardcore runners who believe that running barefoot is the way forward and your best bet in terms of preventing injury. The theory behind the benefits and advantages of barefoot running all stem from the theory that in evolutionary terms we are not designed to wear running shoes but should run barefoot. However, unless the thought of running 5k or 10k with your

feet exposed to the elements floats your boat, and you believe the prospect of treading on broken glass, rusty nails or sharp stones only adds to the 'excitement' of the race, I'd opt for the safe (and sane) option of choosing a sturdy pair of running shoes that will help to cushion the impact of your running stride and keep your feet safe from foreign objects becoming embedded in them.

Which shoe for you?

Whether you look online or visit the high street, the amount of choice you'll face is staggering. There are dozens of brands, shapes, colours, sizes and prices, making the decision to choose just the one pair nearly as daunting as the pending weeks of training. However, there is one fundamental piece of advice you have to follow if you are to give yourself the best possible chance of getting through your training free

Expert corner

According to the Society of Chiropodists and Podiatrists, when you run, your body weight is multiplied three times or more, with your feet and lower limbs bearing the brunt of this stress each and every time they hit the ground. An average-sized man can process approximately 112 tons of weight through each limb for every single kilometre he runs.

Whereas this might lead you to believe that your training regime is going to leave you crippled, rest assured that your body is more than able to tolerate this impact. But, to make its life easier, it's a good idea to ensure you invest in a high-quality specialist running shoe. This will ensure that your feet are well protected from the impact of running on hard surfaces, thereby reducing the effects of shock travelling up your legs and into your lower back.

from niggling joint and muscle pain. Even if you anticipate walking the event, buying a good pair of shoes that are specifically manufactured to absorb shock from hard surfaces will help to protect your joints and make training a far more enjoyable experience.

The relationship between your choice of running shoe and a painful hip or knee soon after you start training might sound a little far-fetched, but it is now recognised by the majority of running injury specialists that the best way to treat most running injuries is to prevent them in the first place, by choosing the correct shoe for your running gait.

What is my running gait?

Put simply, your running gait is the way you run and, ultimately, how your feet act when they hit the ground and propel you forwards as you progress through your running stride.

There are dozens of reasons why our feet land differently when we run, from weak core stability (our inner 'corset' of muscles) to the genes we inherited from our parents, but in order to safeguard against injury, it is essential that you find out what type of running gait you have and buy the appropriate running shoes to complement it.

Get assessed

The first thing you need to do is find a good running store near you and have an expert assess the way you run. After a quick assessment, they will then be able to advise you on the type of running shoe you need. You can be assessed in a number of different ways, including:

- being filmed running on a treadmill;
- having an expert simply watch you run;
- having your feet biomechanically assessed;

- running on a pressure pad that provides feedback on which shoe is most suitable.

There is no 'best' way to get your gait assessed. Despite what some 'experts' might say, as long as you are analysed by a running gait specialist, they will be able to offer sound advice on which trainers you need.

In extreme cases of abnormal lower leg biomechanics such as excessively tight muscles, different leg lengths, or collapsed arches (the base of your feet), you may be advised to seek further professional advice from a foot specialist such as a podiatrist who may prescribe special shoe inserts to place in your trainers.

Whether you have been filmed jogging on a treadmill or had your sweet-smelling feet carefully looked at by a brave lower leg biomechanic, he or she should come to the same conclusion and be able to tell you which one of the following categories you fall into.

- Neutral runner: Your running stride is perfect and you have every right to feel smug. You are the envy of most runners, and are less likely to pick up niggling injuries as this gait places the least amount of stress on the lower leg muscles.

- Over-pronator: Your feet 'roll over' excessively during your running stride and you'll need shoes to provide support to counter this.

- Under-pronator: Although you are the rarest breed of runner, you run more on the outside of your feet and will be recommended trainers to counteract this.

Based on the results of your running gait assessment, you will be given a choice of trainers to choose from and all you have to do is select the shoe that feels the most comfortable and suits your budget. The choice might still be overwhelming, but the advice I have offered my clients over the years on choosing trainers is simple: choose a pair of running shoes that are not only comfortable but are also made by a specialist running shoe manufacturer such as Brooks, Mizuno, Asics, New Balance or Saucony. If you are going to spend the next few months pounding the streets, you need to know that the shoes you are wearing have been made by a reputable company and that they're not going to fall apart on you after just a few weeks.

Over-pronator? You're in good company

It is estimated that about 70 per cent of runners over-pronate – some mildly, some excessively – but the good news is that, because of this, there are a large selection of trainers on the market to choose from.

From the ever popular Brooks Adrenaline to the more timidly named Nike LunarGlide, there are dozens of running shoes to choose from – all you've got to do is find the ones that suit you.

Running attire: high-tech or high street?

If you are one of the many thousands of new runners who, on entering an event, has raided their wardrobe and discovered that their current selection of running kit is bordering on being classed as fancy dress, it's probably time to invest in some new gear.

As with any other pastime or sport, it's very easy to be seduced by the big brand names, all trying to convince you to buy their new special tops/trousers and socks etc., but ultimately the most important consideration is whether the clothes fit properly and are going to be suitable for the time of year you're going to be training.

Tops and vests

The vast majority of 5k and 10k events are held in the spring, summer and autumn, so if there's only one piece of high-tech running kit you buy, I'd suggest

'We found that training together for the Bupa 10k was a great way to keep motivated. Fitting training runs around a busy work and social life isn't always easy, but teaming up really helped to make training fun – despite the occasional bickering!'

Shirin and Mark Pawlowska

you look into getting yourself a good running T-shirt or vest.

Although the marketing is laid on pretty thick for running products to make it sound as though you'd melt in your own body heat if you didn't use one of their tops, they are actually all incredibly effective at keeping you as cool as possible during a run.

One leading manufacturer, for example, has a range of running tops that have undetectable metal fibres embedded in the cloth, which transfer warm air from the skin to the outside of the fabric, keeping you dry and helping to better regulate your body temperature on a hot day. Of course, you have to pay a premium for such tops, but if you anticipate spending the next few months running in the heat, one or two of these might come in handy.

Whether you opt for a high-tech top or a baggy T-shirt to run in, the most important thing you need to consider is the fit. All tops are mass produced and cut to a certain shape, so before you commit to buying one make sure that it fits well and doesn't feel excessively tight round the armpits.

Although some high-tech tops are fitted and meant to cling to the body without the risk of rubbing, cotton tops in particular can chafe the area under the arm quite badly if the fabric is too close to the skin, and this can get very painful during a long run.

As unpleasant as it is, sadly there are also going to be days when it's pouring with rain and your schedule is telling you that you've got to take on a long run. Running in the rain is not as bad as you think. Once you're wet you're wet, and after a while you actually forget about it. Waterproof running jackets can be a worthwhile investment to keep you dry, but make sure they are lightweight and fit well.

Shorts and trousers

As with tops, it's essential that what you wear on the lower part of your body fits well and is not likely to rub.

There is a wide selection of shorts, half, three-quarter and full-length running trousers on the market, but ultimately it's very much down to personal preference. If you opt for high-tech running trousers, you'll see that they are all fairly figure hugging, which may make them comfortable and reduce the risk of rubbing, but the downside is whether you feel confident wearing them. Lots of runners feel a little self-conscious in bum-hugging polyester and spandex trousers, so it really is up to you – opt for whatever you feel comfortable wearing.

However, the word comfort should not be taken too literally and see you opting for a pair of denim shorts. Make sure you choose a pair of running trousers or

Underwear

Deciding what to wear underneath your trousers or shorts is, again, a personal matter, but compression, or 'cycling', shorts are often preferred by most runners. Try to avoid tight cotton underwear, though, as this is a first-class ticket to rubbing sensitive areas when they get sweaty – a situation best avoided if you want to enjoy your training and racing.

shorts which are designed specifically for running and will let your legs breathe and won't become uncomfortable and start rubbing halfway through a training run.

Accessories

Although your trainers, tops and trousers are the items on show, there are a number of other bits and pieces that are often overlooked but are, in fact, just as important.

Socks

Running socks are essential to help prevent blisters – one of the runner's most frustrating ailments. Although in some cases blisters are very hard to avoid, especially when running in new trainers, a good-quality pair of running socks are very effective at reducing the amount of rubbing on the soft skin of your feet. Running socks are dual layered and made out of a special fabric designed to be kind to your feet by wicking away moisture to prevent rubbing and the formation of blisters.

As you'll read later, prevention is always better than cure and this is particularly the case with blisters. As soon as the skin is aggravated and a blister begins to form, running will only make it worse and it can take days before the skin hardens up again. Although it might be difficult to bring yourself to shell out £10 on a pair of socks, the investment will be well worth it. Any runner will tell you that blisters are the bane of their life, yet they are one occupational hazard that can easily be avoided.

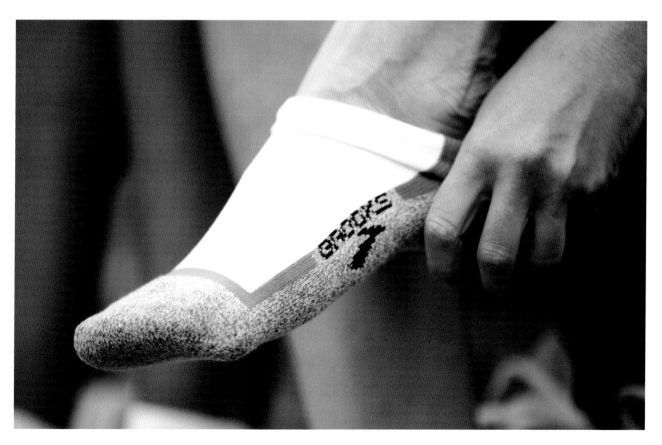

Hat and gloves

If your months of training fall in the winter, then a pair of gloves and a hat will help to keep the chill off, particularly if you suffer from cold extremities.

Hats are not always essential, particularly if you have a good head of hair, but they can help to keep you warm on particularly chilly days, for a solid physiological reason. Newborn babies don't wear hats just to look cute in photos, but because this helps to retain 50 per cent of their body heat, which is emitted from their heads. Although as adults we're able to better regulate our temperature, if you feel the cold more than most, then a beanie hat big enough to cover your ears will make your training session a lot more enjoyable and a lot less cold.

As for your hands and fingers, gloves are a welcome accessory. When you exercise, blood is diverted away from areas that aren't being used and channelled to the working muscles in your legs, leaving your hands particularly prone to feeling the chill of the winter air.

Of course, the options are endless for which type of gloves you choose, but for those who couldn't possibly head out for a training session without their touch-screen iPod, some manufacturers have now designed gloves with a special pad on the finger tips, which means you can play with functions and skip songs without taking your gloves off!

Music

Knowing where to keep your iPod or MP3 player whilst out running can be tricky, especially if the kit you have invested in doesn't have many pockets. Luckily most good running stores (or good old Google) can find you a suitable arm strap with transparent screen in which to house your iPod. This not only gives you the luxury of being able to fast-forward songs without having to dig around in your pockets, but it also stops it jumping around in your pocket which can get really annoying.

Money holder

Although many runners use their socks to store their emergency tenner, a 30-minute sweaty jog during your lunch break in July is a good way to reduce it back to pulp and render it useless. More often than not, if you've invested in a branded make of running shorts or trousers, you'll find that somewhere there is a tiny zip (usually at the back or the side) that will open up a pocket for you to keep a note and/or a few coins in.

Water bottle

Incredibly useful when running in warm weather, a specialist running bottle which you can easily fit in your hand is a great accessory to have. Its contents might be on the warm side after 30 minutes, but you'll welcome the occasional slurp of water or juice on a warm day.

Case study

Name: Emily Hutchison

Age: 31

Occupation: Marketing Consultant

Years of running experience: Seven

Although I'd be the first to admit that my running regime is somewhat irregular, when I get in a routine and run regularly, I feel so much better about myself.

The first real race I entered was the 2004 London Marathon (I must have been mad) and despite all the hard months running in rubbish weather, it has never put me off slipping my trainers back on and heading out for a stress-busting jog.

If there was one thing I learnt from my marathon training days, it was realising just how important it was to wear the right clothes for the conditions. Whatever distance I run now, from a 5k to a 10k (I haven't been brave enough to do a marathon again!), I check the temperature outside so I know how many layers to put on, or leave off.

There is nothing worse than wearing the wrong clothes. Jogging in the early days was tough enough, but it was even worse when I got soaked to the skin and freezing cold just because I didn't equip myself with the right running gear. And it doesn't stop at clothing. Just a few weeks before running the marathon I decided to switch trainers to avoid my training blisters getting worse on the big day. Big mistake! Despite transferring the insoles, the new trainers proved too small and by mile 26, I had lost most of my toe nails!

Once I realised (despite my cynicism) that good quality running gear actually does make a difference, I found that I was able to run further, harder and for longer. Now I always get my trainers fitted at a specialist running shop to make sure they fit properly, suit my running gait ... and look after those toe nails.

3

run to the beat

Contrary to popular belief, using a heart rate monitor during your training is neither as complicated nor as expensive as you might think. After your trainers and clothes, a heart rate monitor should feature as the next most important item in your running wardrobe, to help keep your training on track and ensure you are running within your limits.

For every one of my years as a personal trainer, I have strongly believed in the importance of knowing how the heart responds to exercise, for both safety and fitness-monitoring purposes. Being aware of how hard your heart is working on each training walk, jog or run, you can have peace of mind that you are not over-working (or under-working) your cardiovascular system and you have real-time feedback, so you know when to ease off the pace or even put your foot down.

It is a common myth that the use of heart rate monitors is reserved for the more serious athlete and that you have to remortgage your house to purchase one. Even if you anticipate walking and jogging a 5k course, a heart monitor costing less than half the price of a pair of running shoes can quickly become your best friend, and will help give you peace of mind that you are training at just the right intensity.

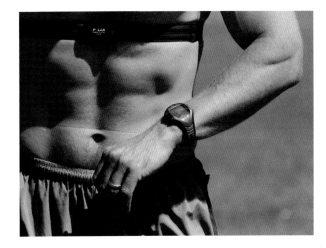

Expert corner

Personal trainers are not alone in believing that monitoring your heart rate during exercise can be incredibly beneficial. Fotini Rozakeas, a British Heart Foundation Nurse, states that 'By monitoring your heart rate, you can use it as a guide to ensure that you are achieving the benefits of moderate-intensity, aerobic exercise such as brisk walking, cycling or jogging. This amount of activity will help to protect you against cardiovascular disease and will help protect your heart.'

❖heart monitoring: the basics

Your heart is, without question, the most valuable organ in your body. It works every minute of every hour of every day, and it has an unenviable job description. Just some of the heart's jobs include:

- pumping the blood through 60,000 miles of blood vessels;
- beating approximately 100,000 times every day, or 35,000,000 million times a year;
- pumping 14,000 litres of blood around the body every day.

These everyday physiological processes are of course beyond your control, but while you're out training, by keeping tabs on your heart rate using a monitor, you are in a position to better regulate how hard your heart works during your workout.

The big question is, how hard should you be making your heart work in order to help improve your fitness? And, to be on the safe side, how hard is too hard?

The heart's the limit

A normal resting heart rate is anywhere from 60–80 beats per minute. This can vary massively depending on fitness levels (the higher your resting heart rate, the more unfit you are) and genetics, but the majority of people fall within this range. The best time to get an accurate reading of your resting heart rate is first thing in the morning when you are relaxed and heart rate raising adrenaline has not had a chance to kick in.

Your maximum heart rate (known as 'HR max') is also variable, depending on a number of factors, but the most reliable factor is your age. Again, there is a degree of variability from person to person but, as a rough guide, the maximum number of times your heart can beat per minute can be determined by subtracting your age from 220 if you are male and 226 if you are female.

Example

If you are a 40-year-old woman, your maximum possible heart rate is:

$$226 - 40 = 186$$

If you are a 40-year-old man your maximum possible heart rate is:

$$220 - 40 = 180$$

It is from this figure that you can then work out how hard you should be running during your training runs. You do this by exercising at a certain percentage of your maximum heart rate – a term commonly referred to as your suggested 'heart rate zone'.

Table 3.1 Maximum possible heart rate

Age	Male	Female
20	200	206
30	190	196
40	180	186
50	170	176
60	160	166
70	150	156

What is your training zone?

Ok, so you've worked out your maximum heart rate, now all you need to do is work out your training zones – which is far easier than it sounds.

Put simply, during your training you are going to need to run at certain intensities so that you can make the necessary fitness gains to achieve your

The HR max formula

There is much debate about how to find out your true HR max, with some experts casting considerable doubt over the accuracy of the '220/226 minus your age' formula to work out your maximum heart rate. Research on heart rate training by leading exercise physiologists Jack Wilmore and David Costill in their book *Physiology of Sport and Exercise* (Human Kinetics) has suggested that, for 95 per cent of 40 year-olds, the maximum heart rate falls in the range of 156–192bpm.

So, by all means use the formula as a guide, but feel free to adjust it if you feel your theoretical HR max is a little on the low side.

race goal. When you're training with a heart monitor, these intensities are shown as percentages of your maximum heart rate, and generally fall between 70 and 90 per cent of it.

So, imagine you're a 40-year-old woman with a maximum heart rate of 186 – now let's work out how many beats per minute (bpm) your heart should be making during training runs.

Gentle zone: 60–70 per cent

If you are new to exercise and haven't done much in the way of physical activity for a few years and/or feel you are carrying a little more weight than you'd like, it's a good idea to train in your gentle zone for a week or two, just to get your heart accustomed to exercise again.

Although you have the option to up your pace a notch whenever you feel ready, if you are starting from scratch I recommend that, for the first two or three weeks, every time the training schedule recommends you go for a jog, you run in your 'gentle zone'.

Your gentle heart rate zone is a heart rate that is generally in the region of 60–70 per cent of your maximum heart rate. So:

60–70 per cent of 186 = between 111 and 130bpm

Which means that you should be aiming to keep your heart rate no higher than 130bpm and no less than 111bpm. For some people, this intensity might seem too gentle, but if you are unsure and are a little anxious about undertaking the upcoming weeks of training, this zone is ideal to start off with.

Jogging zone: 70–75 per cent

For many runners, the jogging zone is where you will be spending the majority of your training weeks. It is a pace at which you should still be able to hold a conversation with someone, and it should feel 'comfortable' and not a speed that you feel is overly fast or unsustainable. So:

70–75 per cent of 186 = 130–139 bpm

By keeping your heart rate between 130 and 139bpm, your body will be working at just the right intensity to adapt to the stresses of training and, over time, this will make your heart stronger and more efficient.

Running zone: 75–85 per cent

Now we're getting into the tough part of training. Running at this intensity is difficult to maintain for a long period of time if you are not used to it, so be cautious if you are new to running and you find your heart rate creeping up to and over the 75 per cent barrier.

The difficulty of running at this intensity is offset by the immense fitness gains that can be made by regular training sessions performed in your running heart rate zone. You might find yourself sweating profusely and panting like there's no tomorrow but the hard work really does pay off. So:

75–85 per cent of 186 = 139–158bpm

Initially, running at 85 per cent of your HR max will not feel pleasant, but you will adapt over time and see significant improvements in your running ability.

Advanced running zone: 85–95 per cent

Unless you have been running or exercising rigorously for a few months, it's best to avoid training with your heart rate this high. Going from a sedentary lifestyle where your heart rate barely exceeds 90 beats a minute, to then making it pump at over 90 per cent of its maximum ability puts it under enormous stress, and it can be dangerous.

Running at this intensity can be performed only in short bursts, and is best undertaken during special training sessions known as 'interval training' (this is explained in more detail in the next chapter).

Exercising this hard once or twice a week can give you massive fitness gains, but you pay the price in terms of increased risk of injury and the discomfort that this intensity of running can inflict on your leg

A cautionary note

It is extremely important that you consult your GP if you are currently taking any medication for high blood pressure or angina, particularly if you intend to use a heart rate monitor throughout your training. Certain prescription medications for these conditions are known as beta-blockers and work by stopping your heart from beating too fast. If this applies to you, then it is dangerous to follow the above heart rate zone guidelines – it is best to ask your doctor what heart rate limits are best for you and your condition.

muscles. Unless you have a specific goal to achieve on race day, or you are a glutton for punishment, I'd leave this intensity well alone and enjoy your training in the relative comfort of your jogging zone. So:

85–95 per cent of 186 = 158–176bpm

the heart of the matter: what sort of monitor should you choose?

The decision of whether to use a heart rate monitor to help you prepare for your chosen event is of course totally up to you. Some runners love them and find it difficult to train without them, others see them as a waste of time and just enjoy running as far and as fast as they like without feeling compelled to check their heart rate every few minutes.

Most popular models of heart rate monitors come in two parts – the watch receiver and the chest transmitter. The transmitter fits snugly around the chest near the breastbone and sends a radio signal to the watch receiver on the wrist watch.

Designs have improved dramatically over the years and although the thought of putting an elasticated strap around your chest sounds uncomfortable, you'll forget it's there once you start running. With a range of models available on the market, some of which are multi-functional and not only measure your heart rate but also how far and fast you are running, there is a heart rate monitor to suit the needs and budgets of everyone.

However, if you're dabbling with the idea of investing in one but worried about the cost, why not just do what nearly all 21st-century shoppers seem

Leading heart rate monitor manufacturer Polar produces a series of entry-level models, which are both easy to use and – more importantly – easy on the wallet. They feature all the functions you will need to see you through your training. These include:

- Heart rate
- Average heart rate
- Stopwatch function
- Percentage of maximum heart rate function
- Calories burned

Most models should have these features and, although you can buy very cheap models that will only give you your current heart rate, just a few of the additional features can be really helpful.

Average heart rate

Knowing what your average heart is after a training session can be a really good way of charting your

'I felt naked if I went out for a training run without my heart rate monitor. Although I splashed out on a top of the range Polar monitor with GPS tracking, I'd recommend all runners invest in one, even if it is a basic model.'

Michael Lock

to be doing these days: Google 'heart rate monitor' and see what you find.

The range of monitors you can buy is extensive, so the model you choose is ultimately down to what you want to use it for, how fat your wallet is and how resistant you are to being seduced by highly functional (yet often unnecessary) gadgetry.

Although certain models, such as Garmin, come with high-tech GPS (useful if you want to know how far you've run), computer link-up and running speed functions, for the majority of runners all you really need from a monitor are the basic functions, which are standard on most entry-level models anyway.

progress, and will give you clear feedback on how your fitness levels are improving. Over time, your thrice-weekly training runs will gradually strengthen your heart muscle, and it will become far more efficient at pumping blood to the working muscles.

This extra strength and efficiency makes the training runs that initially found you gasping for air far easier, and the proof is right there on your heart rate monitor: your heart is not having to work nearly as hard as it did just a few weeks ago.

For example, if the very first training session you took on involved a gentle 2k jog, it's very possible that your unconditioned heart may have been going like the clappers and averaged a high heart rate of 150, or as much as 80 per cent of your HR max.

However, after as little as two weeks of training your heart will have adapted to increased activity levels and will find the same run at the same speed a piece of cake – and it is highly likely that your average heart rate will have dropped down to 140, or 75 per cent of your HR max. This is a far more sustainable rate, and one that won't make you feel nearly as exhausted.

By keeping tabs on your average heart rate, you'll be amazed at how uplifting it can be to watch it drop as you continue through your training programme, and you'll look back in disbelief in months to come at just how hard you were making your heart work to jog such a short distance.

Stopwatch

Having an integrated stopwatch on your heart monitor makes sense as it means you don't have to carry a separate time-measuring device with you and you can easily keep an eye on how long you have been running. For runners who are aiming to finish a 5k or 10k under a certain time, this is particularly important as you can easily check how fast you are running each kilometre, while at the same time

ensuring that you are running in your correct heart rate zone.

Percentage of maximum heart rate

For those training runs where it's advised that you should keep your heart rate within a certain training zone – 70–75 per cent of HR max, for example – there is a function on some watches that can display at what percentage of your maximum heart rate you are training, rather than the actual rate. This can be particularly useful if, like me, you keep forgetting what your heart rate should be during a long run and instead find it easier to just check that you are working at 70–75 per cent of HR max. It's not essential, but some runners find it a useful feature.

Calories

Although the number of calories you burn on every training run is not particularly relevant to how well you are conditioning your body, it can be incredibly satisfying to watch your calorie count accumulate during a run or during the week. Some runners will use their 'calories burned' figure to justify a rewarding glass of Pinot Grigio at the end of the week, and although on a professional level I should encourage you to opt for water instead, why not treat yourself to one of your vices once in a while – life is for living!

Keep a training diary

Keeping a training diary with information about every training run is a fantastic way to track your improvements and keep a log of heart rate information. For each training run, bullet point details of your run so you can refer back to them and see how much you have come on. A typical entry might look like this:

Route: *Three laps around the park*

Time: *34 minutes*

Average heart rate: *156*

Conditions: *Pretty warm – about 23°C*

Calories burned: *340*

Notes: *Felt pretty good until the last 500 metres, where I upped the pace and felt pooped at the end. A lot of eye candy out today so will definitely run the same route next time!*

Making these easy-to-jot-down notes straight after a run is a great motivator and highly rewarding when you see how many calories your training helps you to burn off every week and how much easier you start to find your training runs.

'*Always have a goal to aim for, such as a 10k run or a Race for Life event as it adds so much more purpose to your training. Always start your training off slowly and don't be afraid to walk – it's easy to be put off if you got at it too hard early on.*'

Carol Brewer and her daughter Laura Brewer

∴heart's all a flutter: be aware of the variables

Without doubt, using a heart rate monitor throughout your training preparation can be an invaluable tool, if you follow the guidelines provided and always train within your limits.

However, seeing that we're essentially analysing cardiovascular feedback from our highly unpredictable and changeable bodies, there are a few variables that can have a huge impact on your heart rate, and if you are not aware of them they could completely throw you and cause concern that something is wrong with your heart.

Table 3.2 Reasons for high heart rate

Stimulus	Reason	Expected HR increase
Coffee	Makes the body produce extra adrenaline, which stimulates the heart rate to increase	Highly variable due to individual responses to caffeine; an increased rate of 5 beats at rest is normal
Heat	A warm environment pushes the blood to the surface of the skin to cool the body; this process causes the heart to pump faster	Depends on how hot it is, but resting and exercising HR can increase by well over 10 beats
Stress	Like caffeine, stress can stimulate the adrenal glands to secrete more adrenaline, which acts as a stimulant to the heart	Depends on the amount of stress, but expect 5–10 beats extra. If you are chronically stressed, seek advice from your GP
Excitement/anticipation	Before a race or build-up to a tough training run, the anticipation of exercise again stimulates the adrenal glands to secrete extra adrenaline	Varies hugely. Expect an increased HR of at least 5–10 beats, but I have witnessed first hand an increase of 50 beats, just standing and mentally preparing for a hard session
Oncoming cold/virus	Viral infections can elevate resting heart rate even if you are not experiencing symptoms	Expect a resting heart rate increase of 5–10 beats
Subtle incline during a run	Even a small, nearly unnoticeable incline during a run can elevate heart rate, so if in doubt look behind you and see if you can spot that you're running uphill – albeit a small one	Hills can easily add 5–10 beats on top of your normal exercising heart rate
No obvious reason	If you notice your heart rate is up for an unexplained reason, seek professional advice from your GP as soon as possible	Anything higher than 10 beats of your usual resting heart rate, you're best to get seen to if you feel unwell

Like nearly all of your other organs, glands and cells, your heart is highly responsive to a variety of nutritional, emotional and environmental stimuli, which can result in massive fluctuations in what is considered to be your 'normal' resting or training heart rate.

Without being aware that something as seemingly innocent as a cup of coffee can elevate your resting and training heart rate, you might think that something was wrong and start to worry. So, to put your mind at rest, the table above highlights some of the most common reasons why your heart rate, both at rest and during exercise, might be a little higher than is considered 'normal'.

Case study

Name: Simon Vittle

Age: 33

Occupation: Client Relations Manager

Years of running experience: 10

Ever since I started running, I have always had a problem knowing how to pace myself. Maybe it's the competitive instinct of being a bloke, but over the years I have always found it really difficult to know what pace to run at, during training and during a race.

The one thing that has been invaluable to me to help address this is the use of a heart rate monitor. Following advice from a personal trainer, I am now able to use my heart rate to help gauge my pace and prevent me from over pacing and conking out after just 10 minutes. I now know that if my heart rate exceeds a certain level for even just minutes, I'll pay for it later on in the run.

The heart rate monitor has also been great for harder training runs, too, not just the gentle ones. I was introduced to the 'heart rate game' by a personal trainer where you run at a fast pace until your heart reaches a certain level (175 for me), then slow down until it drops to a lower level (140 for me) and then run hard again. It makes a run much more interesting and although it's hard work, this game has always helped me improve my running fitness.

My advice to any runner starting to run (or even if you've been running for years) is to look into buying a heart rate monitor and use it on every training run you do. I now find it really difficult to run without one and if I do (although I'm better than I was) I still find myself running too fast and making what should be a gentle and enjoyable jog into an exhausting and less pleasurable workout.

preparing for training

For those of you who are new to the world of running, the prospect of exchanging your usual weekly routine of coming home from work, putting your feet up in front of the TV, for one that features up to four training runs every week for 10–12 weeks can be intimidating. Even for the more competitive runners who are hell bent on finishing their chosen event in a personal best time, beginning any training programme is always difficult.

Whatever aspirations you have for your chosen 5k or 10k race, be it the sub-60-minute 10k or just to complete the course in one piece, the long weeks of training leading up to the event will ultimately determine how much you enjoy the race day experience and maybe help you make the decision as to whether you want to do it all over again some time.

Your training preparations should ideally start as soon as you have secured your place in the event, giving you a good three months of preparation to condition your heart, legs and lungs to be able to tolerate the demands of running in an event lasting anywhere from 30 minutes to an hour and a half or more.

This chapter addresses the best way to approach your training regime, and gives you a number of tips on how to get the most out of your training and, above all, enjoy it.

⁘running: revitalising the mind, body and soul

However fast or slowly you choose to run, running can be incredibly therapeutic and a fantastic escape from the stresses and strains of everyday life.

A forest trail, a canal towpath or even the open road can help give you a brief respite away from everyday anxieties such as financial concerns and emotional worries, giving you time out to refresh your mind, body and soul. As tedious and mundane as you think 12 weeks of training might be right now, after just a few sessions you'll come to realise just how fulfilling your training sessions can be and, before you know it, you'll be dying to get out there to offload some pent-up emotional baggage.

Many new runners who discover how effective training can be as a great stress reliever often dub their training sessions 'me time', and find that just three short sessions every week keep their heads clear and them in a far better frame of mind to take on whatever life throws at them – be it their boss, their kids or other (demanding) half.

It may come as little surprise that large chunks of this book have effectively been written while I was out running and in desperate need of some inspiration. Running gives you time to think, and it's amazing how effective even a short jog can be in helping to give you clarity of thought and a renewed and more positive outlook on life.

Expert corner

Leading mental health charity Mind knows all too well the positive effect that training for a 5k or 10k event can have. Its chief executive Paul Farmer, explains: 'It's a well-known fact that exercise is good for your physical health, but people can be surprised to hear that it's great for your mental health too. In the short term it can help you sleep better, feel less tense or stressed, and also give you more energy. In the long run a programme of moderate exercise, such as gently training for a 5k race, will help you feel better about yourself, and reaching a goal will boost your self esteem and confidence, all of which contribute to good mental well-being.'

the first run

Often the hardest of all the training runs is your very first one, not only physically but mentally too.

Whether you are reading this on the eve of your first training run, or even in the minutes before you head out the front door, many new runners find themselves behaving like award-winning procrastinators when it comes to their very first run. Taking those first intrepid steps can take a long time.

Although some runners will be full of zest and enthusiasm to get their training regime under way, there are those who are a little more wary of what the next 12 or so weeks of regular training have in store, and it can be a nervy time.

Just a few of the anxieties I have had to address over the years with first-time runners include:

- How do I run?
- How do I breathe?
- Will the training be uncomfortable?
- Do I need to stretch and, if so, how do I stretch?
- What should I eat before exercise?

All of these concerns are addressed throughout this chapter and the remaining chapters of the book, so if you tick any of the above boxes, be assured that your worries will be dealt with and your training anxieties allayed.

what type of runner are you?

Virgins

If you are a first timer or novice runner, whose focus is more geared to finishing the course than crossing

'*I love complementing my running training within the gym environment for convenience and social reasons. You can also monitor your pace and performance against set targets.*'

David Durston

the line first, your mindset for your first few weeks of training should be nothing more than gaining maximum enjoyment from each session.

You might not have a specific time in mind, or even be too bothered if you end up walking half of the course, but to assist you with your training, it really helps if you set yourself some sort of goal to aim for on race day or throughout your training regime.

Giving yourself a goal or two to aim for, however menial or uncompetitive they might seem to some more serious runners, is so important in helping to keep you motivated and focused on your training regime, and can really help you to gain maximum satisfaction and a sense of achievement once you cross that line.

Here are just a few examples of some of the training and race-day goals that some of my previous clients have aimed for.

- Aim to always train no fewer than three times a week (unless you are ill).

- Aim to raise £500 for your chosen charity.

- Burn at least 1,000 (for 5k training) or 2,000 (for 10k training) running calories a week.

- Finish the race without walking one step.

Whatever goal(s) you choose to set yourself, they can really help to give you a reason to slip your running shoes on when it's blowing a gale or raining stair rods and you are in desperate need of some motivation to take to the road.

Experienced and competitive

For those who have already completed a few 5k and 10ks, and for whom finishing isn't the issue, but finishing fast is, getting your mindset right from day one of training is really important. Your first day and first week of training can dictate how the rest of your training goes, so make sure you approach it with realistic expectations.

Even though you might already have a good level of fitness and feel that the upcoming weeks of training are just a case of 'going through the motions', be careful not to get over-complacent about how important the correct types of training are in your programme. It's not uncommon for seasoned and competent runners to fall into one of two categories:

1 Under-train in the belief that their last personal best will be easy to beat.

2 Over-train and push too hard to achieve an unrealistic goal, and end up getting injured and missing a couple of weeks of training.

Despite my many years of experience as a runner, I have fallen into both of these training traps at least once, most notably in my effort to break the elusive 35-minute barrier for 10k, which highlights the danger that even the most experienced of runners can lose sight of sensible training practices. (For the record, a sub-35-minute 10k still eludes me.)

⠿keep it real: aim for an achievable goal

Although your ultimate goal for the weeks of training ahead, and the race itself, is to get under a certain time, keep it realistic and aim for a goal you know is achievable. Entering a race that is marketed as flat and fast may very well get the competitive juices flowing and make you think that you'll easily be able to knock three minutes off your PB – but do the maths.

Three minutes might not sound very much, but when you consider that you'll have to run each

kilometre 35 seconds faster over 5k and 18 seconds faster over 10k, to achieve that goal in real terms isn't that easy.

By all means aim high and strive to achieve a challenging goal, but throughout your training make sure you keep tabs on how fast you are running each kilometre, and if by halfway through your training, that extra 35 seconds of extra speed per kilometre is proving too much, simply adjust your goal to a more realistic one.

Run for enjoyment and fulfilment, not for torment and disappointment.

⠿technique

For those who have run for years, the motion of a running stride might very well feel like a natural instinct, but for many people for whom this might be their first event, the question of 'How exactly do you run?' is perfectly justifiable.

The issue of what to do with your arms, how to breathe and where to look can leave people in utter confusion and dominate their minds for the first few weeks of training. Any enjoyment you should be getting from your training experience can instead be lost in worrying about looking like a plonker, and being concerned that your arms and legs are flailing all over the shop and you look more like a character from a Monty Python sketch.

First, it is perfectly normal to have these concerns, and you certainly won't be the only one worried about your running style. Although it might not feel like it initially, running is a very natural movement and, while you might feel a little odd, the action of running will eventually become second nature and you'll notice that in actual fact you look just like any other runner who has been running for years – albeit a little more out of breath in the early stages.

That said, there are four questions that have cropped up countless times over the years from new runners; we will now look at each of these in turn.

1. How should I breathe?

Perhaps the most popular question of all is 'How should I breathe during a run?' With the heart beating twice as hard as it is used to and your rate of breathing going like the clappers, trying to think about what breathing pattern to stick to can be tricky and incredibly distracting. The simple way to get around the breathing issue is, quite simply, do not think about it at all.

Breathing is a natural instinct that your body will do for you without you even thinking about it. You did

Breathing through the nose

Although most runners now realise that it is a myth, for years many recreational joggers believed that the way to breathe was in through the nose and out through the mouth. The reasons for this vary, but if you think about it, trying to draw in large quantities of air through the narrow nasal channel defies logic. Try the following exercise.

- Take a really deep breath in through your nose, quickly, as you would if you were running along and getting out of breath.

- Now, take another deep breath in, quickly, but this time through your mouth.

Which was easier?

It's not even close. You'll find that when you're out running and you start to get breathless, your body will naturally want to draw in as much air as it can and it will automatically choose mouth breathing as its preferred channel.

Breathing through the nose certainly helps to filter out any dust particles in the air, and helps to warm it up as it travels to the lungs, but as far as function is concerned, the idea that air through the nose is more oxygenated than through the mouth is hogwash.

it immediately when you were born, you do it in your sleep, so it stands to reason that your body will breathe as and when it wants to when you're out running. Focusing too hard on a specific breathing pattern while running can make the whole process unnatural, so try not to concentrate on your breathing too much and let your body do it for you.

2. How should my foot land?

Although there are many biomechanical reasons why a runner's (or walker's) foot lands the way it does during a stride (most of which are beyond the scope of this book), the one key thing you need to remember is to run in a way in which you feel most comfortable.

As you run, your foot should naturally land on the outside of the heel and gradually role inwards slightly as you progress through the motion – but this is not always the case. Although, as explained earlier, there are measures you can take to counteract excessive rolling of the foot (over-pronation) by choosing the right type of running shoes (see pages 10–12), the way you run is ultimately an individual one and should feel natural.

Expert corner

According to Dave Dunning, a podiatric biomechanics lecturer/practitioner at Stafford-shire University and a member of the Society of Chiropodists and Podiatrists, the foot is arguably the most complicated organ in the human body: 'The foot is highly adaptive and has a highly developed proprioceptive system (proprioception is best described as a 'sixth sense' that your body and brain uses to know where you are in relation to the world) that is constantly updating the muscles, ligaments, joints etc. [according to] the terrain, with the heel playing a key role in gathering this information, i.e. knowing where you are in space. My advice for runners of any ability is to follow a gait pattern that suits the individual, the activity and the terrain.'

3. Why do I get so out of breath?

The sensation of breathlessness for new runners can initially feel a little uncomfortable, but it doesn't take long before your cardiovascular system adapts to your increased requirement for oxygen and the feeling of breathlessness reduces dramatically. Put in a few kilometres and all of a sudden jogging becomes easy. However, there are cases where runners can find themselves excessively gasping for air after just a few hundred yards no matter how many training runs they do, which can very quickly take away the enjoyment of running and potentially put you off it altogether.

There are two common reasons why you might feel more out of breath than you should do during your first few weeks of training, and luckily there are often simple solutions to both problems.

Speedy Gonzalez

When you first start running, it can be difficult to know how to pace yourself properly and stick to a jogging pace that is within your physiological means. It is common for new runners who begin training for an event to fall into the trap of letting their enthusiasm get the better of them and they set off for a 'gentle'-paced jog at a speed that would impress Usain Bolt. Over the years, I have trained dozens of new runners who were getting despondent at their inability to run for any distance before feeling exhausted, only to realise that they were simply running far quicker than their heart, lungs and legs were able to sustain.

The important part of training for a 5k or 10k is, first and foremost, to make sure you are capable of jogging for long periods of time, with the emphasis on speed coming later in the programme. So, if you find yourself getting excessively out of breath in the early stages of training, try dropping your speed a notch or two and you'll notice a big difference. When it comes to 5k and 10k training, speed is not always of the essence.

Exercise-induced asthma

If you think your running speed is about right but you still find yourself gasping for air after a few weeks of training, there is a chance you might be suffering from a form of asthma – in particular, 'exercise-induced asthma'.

Although it is still unknown exactly why exercise can trigger asthma, leading charity Asthma UK believes that when people exercise and they breathe faster, this makes it more difficult for the nose and upper airways to warm and add moisture to the air breathed in, resulting in the air being drier and colder than usual. It is thought that this cold, dry air in the airways triggers the symptoms of exercise-induced asthma. These include:

- Coughing
- Wheezing
- Tightness in the chest
- Difficulty breathing

These symptoms often present themselves after exercise, and can get worse 15 minutes after exercise has stopped.

If you suffer any of these symptoms, it is strongly advised that you visit your GP. Asthma is a very manageable condition and provided you seek medical advice and are treated accordingly, there is no reason why it should interfere with your training. If Paula Radcliffe can win races and run marathons at an astonishing speed as an asthma sufferer, it proves that it needn't hinder your race preparations.

4. How should I run?

Running should feel natural and the big mistake many people make is to think about it too much. However, the key points to remember when jogging are to run tall, avoiding slouching forwards and to keep your shoulders nice and relaxed. These two tips alone will reduce any unnecessary tension developing in the shoulders and make your training sessions that much more enjoyable.

let the fun begin

Whether you are relishing the prospect of the upcoming weeks of training or you're in a frozen state of fear, this is where your race day preparations begin. Let the fun commence ...

on your marks: training basics

Exactly how hard and how regularly you choose to train is very much up to you and ultimately dependent on your race aspirations, but the most important part of the training is to start it with the mindset of enjoying it.

This chapter has been written to give you an idea of how far, how fast and how regularly you should be running to get yourself into race shape, but remember that it is just a guide. I cannot stress how important it is to always follow your instincts rather than religiously stick to a structured and regimented training plan.

Life is here to be enjoyed and even though you have committed yourself to a 10- or 12-week training programme, it doesn't mean that life has to stop just because your training schedule says you have to go for a 20 or 30 minute run on a certain day. All too often, for reasons which we either resent or welcome

– be it lunch with the in-laws or a post-party hangover – sticking to a highly structured running timetable is almost impossible over the 10- to 12-week period, so whatever plan you choose to follow, use it as a guide not the gospel.

In an ideal world, all runners planning to take on any race, from a 5k to a marathon, would like a 'silver bullet' training plan that they can follow as closely as possible and know that it will take them from zero to running hero, injury free and in the time they had hoped for.

Sadly, however, no one timetable – no matter how well structured – suits every runner. The best way to make it work for you is to know why you are doing each training run, so that you can work out for yourself if your training is on track. If you know why the timetable is suggesting that you go for a '30-minute jog, with bursts', you're in a far better position to judge for yourself whether you actually need to do it to improve your running, or if you can give it a miss and opt for a day off or a gentle jog instead.

All the different types of training run explained in the following pages are there to help you keep your running training interesting and varied, while at the same (for the more competitive runner) ensure that your cardiovascular system and leg muscles are being overloaded (see below) to make you a faster and more efficient runner.

The three golden rules

Regardless of running ability, in order to help the body adapt to running, you have to 'overload' it steadily over time, so that it slowly adapts to the increased distances and/or speeds you are asking your body to endure. This process is excitingly known as 'progressive overload' and, while it sounds dull, it is perhaps the most fundamental principle you must follow for the duration of your training to get yourself into race shape.

The body is brilliant at adapting to everything we throw at it, from learning mathematics to coping with the loss of one of our senses – so, as far as your body is concerned, adapting to the physiological stresses of running is actually pretty easy. All you need to do, irrespective of your anticipated race time, is to overload your body, in the following three ways:

1 Progressively: Increase your 'long run' distance every week, even if only by 500 metres.

2 Slowly: Resist the temptation to increase your long run by any more than 10–15 per cent of your previous maximum (injury is the most likely outcome if you do).

3 Regularly: By training regularly throughout the week, even if they are short runs, your body will adapt to running faster than you might think.

You'll notice that, in the training timetables that follow, each week your long run on day seven will be marginally longer than it was the week before – far enough to make the body work that little bit harder to encourage the adaptation process, but not so far that your muscles and tendons are put under too much stress by running a distance they are simply not ready to take on yet.

Getting the miles in

Although it is strongly recommended that you increase your long run by no more that 10–15 per cent every week, there are going to be some instances where you'll find yourself with little option but to break this rule and up your long run by more. For runners who either start training late or had to take time out through illness, sometimes you have to take the risk and jump up a bit to keep yourself on track and give you a chance to get the 'miles in.' This is fine if you have to, but understand that you're playing a risky game of 'injury Russian roulette', so be careful.

By following the three key principles of progressive, slow and regular training you'll discover that your running fitness will come on in leaps and bounds in no time at all, keeping you free from annoying injuries and confident that you'll find your 5k or 10k race far easier to complete in your anticipated time.

get set: set your pace

Before you decide which of the 5k or 10k training plans best suits you, I strongly suggest that you read through the following explanations of the different types of training that are involved to get you into race shape. Although you might be tempted to dive head-first into week one, day one of the plan, it's essential that you familiarise yourself with the different types of training that you can integrate into your plans, and understand at what level of intensity you should be aiming to complete each training run. The following sections should help you.

Jog: easy and comfortable

Without a doubt, 'jog' days are welcomed by all runners, regardless of the distance they are training for. By and large, jogging days are enjoyable and ultimately what makes running such a pleasurable pastime.

As you'd expect, a jog should be performed at a pace that you feel is comfortable – nice and easy, and one that shouldn't be leaving you gasping for air before you've reached the end of your road. For new runners, you may find that, at the beginning of your training, even an easy-paced jog can leave you more breathless than you'd like, but over time it will get easier. You might find yourself muttering 'What's easy about it?' for the first few sessions but, by week two or three you can enjoy listening to your MP3 player and taking in your surroundings, without worrying about getting too breathless.

A jogging pace should be:

- performed at around 60–70 per cent of your maximum heart rate;
- run at approximately 50–60 per cent of your maximum running speed;
- run at a pace where you can still hold a conversation with someone.

Expert corner

Remember, that just because the plan suggests heading out for a gentle jog or long jog, it doesn't mean you're a failure if you slow down to a walking pace for a few minutes to catch your breath. There are a number of highly regarded running coaches, such as Ernst Van Aaken, an early proponent of women's running and Olympic 5000m coach, who strongly believed that walking during training runs is almost more effective at boosting fitness levels than jogging the whole way. It helps your body develop 'maximum aerobic development' over a long period, and stops you from excessively exhausting yourself.

So, even though the 'Starting from scratch' plan (see page 46) suggests that you walk for 4 minutes and jog for 1, if you find yourself gasping for air after just 45 seconds of jogging, there's no shame in stopping and walking for a little longer.

Bursts: short and sharp

You'll notice in the training plans that every now and again, particularly in the first few weeks of training, you'll come across a session that suggests you go for a 20-minute or so jog, 'with bursts'. As obscure as this might sound, all it means is that every now and then on your jog, you just up your pace for a short period of time. There are no rules, just increase your pace once in a while to give your fitness a bit of an extra boost.

Bursts should:

• last for around 10 seconds in the early weeks of training, increasing to 30 seconds as your fitness improves;

• be performed every 5 minutes or so, but can be repeated more frequently the fitter you get;

• be a very casual and relaxed introduction to the world of 'interval training' (which is what this is) – burst as fast as you like and whenever you feel like it.

Bursts can be implemented in any training programme and at any stage, so feel free to burst whenever the mood takes you!

Run: upping the pace

The next step up from a jog is a run. Although both terms are very much open to interpretation and vary greatly depending on the ability of the individual, a running pace is one that is slightly quicker than a jog, and requires a little more concentration and effort to maintain the pace.

A running pace should be:

• performed at around 70–80 per cent of your maximum heart rate;

• run at approximately 65–75 per cent of your maximum running speed;

• run at a pace where you can hold a conversation with someone only in brief sentences before you have to take a breath.

New runners will find that a running pace will leave them breathless after a minute or so, whereas regular runners can sustain a running pace for the entire 10k. As a guide, whenever it indicates in the programme that you head out for a run, you should run at an intensity that you feel you could just about sustain for the duration of the session. At the end of the run, you should feel pretty tired and be breathing heavily.

Interval run

The phrase 'interval run' or 'interval training' has long put the fear of God into many a new runner, who has been (falsely) led to believe that these sessions are more painful than childbirth and a darn sight less enjoyable.

Interval running is, quite simply, a form of training whereby you increase the intensity of your run – by running up a hill or upping your pace for a short period of time, followed by a period of light recovery jogging or walking. This sequence is repeated a number of times over a given distance or time.

For example, an interval training session might involve an easy jog for 5 minutes to warm up, followed by a run at 70–80 per cent of your maximum running speed for 60 seconds, followed by a recovery walk for 2 minutes. This is then repeated eight to ten times in the session.

Whereas it might be true that for those runners who are keen to finish the race in a fast time, performing repeated and intense interval runs can be quite unpleasant, it doesn't have to be that way for everyone. Interval runs can be performed at a variety of intensities and needn't be so difficult as to put you off running for life.

Interval runs can in fact be a great way to break away from a conventional steady-paced run and add welcome variety to your weekly training schedule. Some runners actually enjoy interval runs, as the hard work goes in short bursts followed by an enforced walking recovery period.

Although interval runs are not essential, especially if you are not looking to break any land-speed records for the race, I strongly suggest you perform one interval session a week as part of your training regime. Remember, it doesn't have to be lung busting – just fast enough that it makes you work a bit harder than you do during an easy-paced jog.

To take the guesswork out of how intensely you should tackle each interval session, have a look at the examples of interval runs for runners of varying ability on page 42.

Cross-train

Like any sporting activity, doing the same thing over and over again for weeks on end can get a little dull and, before you know it, demotivation can set in and hauling yourself off the sofa and out for a jog can be incredibly difficult. Although some people might have the good fortune to have a loving other half that kicks them out of the front door to go for a run, some might not be so 'lucky', and other incentives are needed. This is where cross-training comes in …

Cross-training is simply another form of pulse-raising exercise other than running, which can be

Table 5.1 Interval runs for beginners and new joggers

Session	Warm-up	Time of interval	Rest period between intervals (gently jog/walk)	Intensity of interval	Number of intervals
1	Gentle jog/ 5 mins walk and stretch	60 seconds	3 minutes	60–80 per cent of maximum speed	6–8
2	Gentle jog/ 5 mins walk and stretch	90 seconds	4 minutes	60–80 per cent of maximum speed	6–8
3	Gentle jog/ 5 mins walk and stretch	2 minutes	5 minutes	60–80 per cent of maximum speed	6–8

Table 5.2 Interval runs for the more competitive runner

Session	Warm-up	Time of interval	Rest period between intervals (gently jog/walk)	Intensity of interval	Number of intervals
1	Gentle jog/ 5 mins walk and stretch	60 seconds	60 seconds	80–90 per cent of maximum speed	8–10
2	Gentle jog/ 5 mins walk and stretch	90 seconds	90 seconds	75–85 per cent of maximum speed	8–10
3	Gentle jog/ 5 mins walk and stretch	2 minutes	90–120 seconds	75–85 per cent of maximum speed	8–10

Remember, these sessions are just a guide and can be adjusted in a number of ways to make them easier – or harder, if you prefer. As your fitness improves as you progress through the programme, you'll find that these sessions get a lot easier and you'll need to make them a little more intense to help improve your fitness levels even further.

If you want to make them more challenging, change one of the variables every couple of weeks or so by:

• increasing the time of the interval by 30 seconds;

• reducing the recovery period by 30 seconds;

• increasing the speed at which you run each interval by 10 per cent;

• increasing the number of intervals for each session by two.

If you really want to make life hard for yourself, you can even run each interval up a hill, or even jog between intervals rather than walking or stopping.

performed outside or even in the gym. Any other activity that gets you out of breath, sweaty and red in the face can be classed as cross-training, and is a great way to break up the weekly grind of pounding the pavements and allowing you to do something different. The most common forms of cross-training include:

- Swimming
- Cycling (indoors or outdoors)
- Rowing
- Aerobics class
- Step machine
- Elliptical cross-trainer

By including one cross-training session in your weekly routine, this will not only give you something different to do, but will also reduce the stresses and strains that are put on your joints and muscles when you are out running three or four times a week. Although a sensible and gradual training regime should not overly stress your joints to the point of pain, for any injury-prone runners, cross-training every week reduces their chances of overworking vulnerable joints. And, with the added benefit of still working your heart and lungs to help improve your fitness, you can see why cross-training is well worth adding to your weekly training regime.

Naturally, the question many runners ask is 'What form of cross-training is best?' To be honest, the simple answer is the form of cross-training that most takes your fancy and that you will enjoy doing. Although certain forms of cross-training are better than others (rowing, for example, is excellent) there is no point in doing it if it's less enticing than lunch

Don't relax

A common mistake is to approach a cross-training sessions with too relaxed an attitude. If you're going for a swim don't cruise up and down the pool and 'holiday swim' as if you were at a Caribbean resort. Try to make sure that whatever form of cross-training you choose, you put a bit of effort into it, and by the end of the session you should be puffed and feel that you have had a good workout.

with the in-laws – if you hate every minute of it you're not going to get the maximum benefit. So, if you like swimming, go for a swim – if you like cycling, go for a bike ride, and so on ...

Whether you stick with the same type of cross-training every week or mix it up a bit, you should use your cross-training sessions to take a break from running and work your body in a different way. It can be fun to do something different, so choose something you enjoy and make your cross-training session work for you in your bid to get race fit.

To give you an idea of how you can use cross training to replace a 30-minute run, use the following table as a guideline:

Table 5.3 Cross training sessions

Discipline	Duration
Cycling	40–45 minute (with hills)
Swimming	30-minute continuous swim, with occasional 1-minute bursts
Indoor rowing	3 sessions of 10–15 minutes (5-minute rest between intervals)
Elliptical cross-trainer	30–40 minute continuous session

6 go! select your training timetable

OK, this is it. It's time to get cracking and get your training under way in preparation for race day in about 12 weeks' time.

In an ideal world, it would be best if you spent a little longer than 10–12 weeks training for your race (especially for those competing in a 10k). However, the training timetables on the following pages are there to help you get through your race preparations in one piece, and to give you the confidence that you can turn up at the start line on race day knowing that you have the fitness to get you through the race.

which timetable to choose?

There is a training timetable for all abilities, from those of you who are first-time runners to those who are looking to break previous personal bests, so flick through and see which plan best suits your ability. Remember that you can always mix and match the training regimes if you are finding that the one you are following is too easy or too hard – all you need to do is swap a session or two over – or, if you are up to it, you can even include an extra run during the week.

'The biggest lesson I have learnt over my 10-year 'running career' is not to over rely on the treadmill when following a training programme. I have made that mistake a number of times and have now learnt my lesson.

I have found that by conditioning the body to run on the smooth and bouncy track of the treadmill, it does not prepare you as well for the harder and more undulating surface you'll be ultimately racing on. It can come as quite shock to your legs and lungs just how much harder it is to run outside than on the treadmill, so unless it's really extreme weather, I try to stick to outdoor running as much as possible to help my body adapt to true racing conditions underfoot.'

Joanna Hayes

The most important thing to remember is to choose a timetable that you feel is most suitable for you and your lifestyle. There is nothing worse than choosing to follow a plan such the '5k PB' only to find that after just two weeks you simply can not find the time to stick to it and you start falling behind schedule. Although you might have had the time and energy to follow the tougher timetable in your youth, the toll that work/family and dare I say age can sadly catch up with you. By all means set yourself a challenge, but try and keep your training aspirations realistic at the same time. Remember, there is always the option of adding an extra session into your week if you have time, but try not to put yourself under unnecessary pressure to juggle an unrealistic training programme with work and family commitments.

'Starting from scratch' plan

For beginners who are starting from absolute scratch, and planning to try to run most, or even the entire, 5k or 10k without stopping, then this starter timetable is ideal for you. It is designed for those of you who have very little experience of physical activity or might be carrying a little more weight than you'd like. It is a gentle introduction that will condition the body to get it used to regular exercise, and is highly adaptable depending on how well your body responds to the training. Feel free to play around with the walking times and jogging times as much as you like by:

- reducing the walking times/increasing the jogging times if you find it too easy;
- increasing/decreasing the number of jogging intervals you do, depending on how tired you feel;
- adding an extra training day if you feel up to it.

This five-week plan will help to build up your fitness to a sufficient enough level where you'll be able to join the start of the 'Novice 5k and 10k' training plan.

It might feel like you have a mountain to climb now, but once you get started the peak of the mountain will move ever closer and will seem far easier to reach than you imagined. Feel free to spend

Training plan 1: Starting from scratch

WEEK	DAY 1	DAY 2	DAY 3	DAY 4	DAY 5	DAY 6	DAY 7
1	30 min quick walk	Rest	4 min walk, 1 min jog (x 4)	Rest	4 min walk, 1 min jog (x 5)	Rest	4 min walk, 1 min jog (x 6)
2	35 min quick walk	Rest	3 min walk, 1 min jog (x 4)	Rest	3 min walk, 1 min jog (x 4)	Rest/40 min quick walk	3 min walk, 1 min jog (x 5)
3	40 min quick walk	Rest	4 min walk, 2 min jog (x 3)	Rest	4 min walk, 2 min jog (x 4)	Rest /45 min quick walk	3 min walk, 2 min jog (x 5)
4	45 min quick walk	Rest	3 min walk, 3 min jog (x 3)	Rest	3 min walk, 3 min jog (x 4)	Rest /45 min gentle walk	3 min walk, 3 min jog (x 5)
5	50 min quick walk	Rest	3 min walk, 3–4 min jog (x 4)	Rest	3 min walk, 3–4 min jog (x 5)	Rest /45 min gentle walk	3 min walk, 4 min jog (x 6)

longer than five weeks on the plan if you feel you need to, all you need to do is to repeat a week every now and again. There is no such thing as taking too long to prepare for the race and the slower your preparation, the less likely you are to get injured. So even if your chosen event is still six months away, there's no reason why you can't start today.

Key points about following the 'Starting from scratch' plan

- Adjust the length of your jog and walk as much as you like, just ensure that you increase the intensity, even if by just by a little, every week.

- Your quick walk should be performed at a pace that is quicker than a stroll but slower than a power walk.

- Feel free to go for a gentle walk on your rest days.

'Novice 5k and 10k' plans

These timetables have been designed especially for those runners for whom this is either their first running event, who just want to get round, or for those who have hectic work and family lives and will find it difficult to stick to a strict and regimented training schedule.

In the 21st century, life seems crammed full of so many things to do that adhering to a stringent training programme week in week out can be incredibly difficult. With this in mind, these training plans give you a good idea of how much running you should be doing, but allow for the occasional session to be missed due to family or work commitments. Of course, the more closely you follow the plan the better prepared your legs will be to tolerate the race, but even if you manage to follow only 80 per cent of the programme, by the end of your training, your fitness will be good enough that you shouldn't

have any problem getting around the course – and enjoying it at the same time.

Key points about following the 'Novice 5k and 10k' plans

For the first four to five weeks, the 5k and 10k novice training plans have been designed to give you a solid base level of fitness, to get your heart, legs and lungs used to exercising. Any session during this time can be substituted for a brisk walk instead of a jog, so do not feel you're a failure if you walk instead of jog – for the whole session or part of the session.

After the first four or five weeks, your body will have adapted to the exercise and you'll find it easier to be able to sustain a jogging pace for longer, so although it is still OK to take walking breaks, try and stick to a jog for as long as you can.

Other key points to remember are as follows:

- All runners adapt to training programmes in very different ways, with some taking a little longer to adapt to running than others. Therefore, follow the guide at your own pace and, if necessary, repeat a week if you feel it is getting too difficult, or walk for longer periods instead of jogging.

- Just because the plan might tell you to do a 'two-minute run' do not feel you have to run excessively quickly, or even do it at all. It might be something you relish doing in your training, which is great, but at the same time, it might be something that you dread. If this is the case, don't feel you have to do it – go for a gentle jog instead. Training is about enjoyment, not dread or fear of certain sessions.

- If you are finding that the training is not challenging enough, by all means add an extra session during the week, run a little faster or 'steal' a training session from the 'Personal best' plan (see pages 52–3).

Training plan 2: Novice 5k

WEEK	DAY 1	DAY 2	DAY 3	DAY 4	DAY 5	DAY 6	DAY 7
1	Rest/30 min walk	5 min jog, 4 min walk (x 2)	Rest	5 min jog, 4 min walk (x 2)	Rest	Rest/30 min walk	6–8 min jog, 5 min walk (x 2)
2	Rest/30 min walk	5 min jog, 4 min walk (x 3)	Rest	5 min jog, 4 min walk (x 3)	Rest	Rest/30 min walk	8–10 min jog, 5 min walk (x 2)
3	Rest/30 min walk	5 min jog, 3 min walk (x 3)	Rest	5 min jog, 3 min walk (x 3)	Rest	Rest/30 min walk	8–10 min jog, 4 min walk (x 2)
4	Rest/30 min walk	5 min jog, 3 min walk (x 4)	Rest	5 min jog, 3 min walk (x 4)	Rest	Rest/30 min walk	10 min jog, 3 min walk (x 2)
5	Rest/30 min cross-train	6–8 min jog, 3 min walk (x 3)	Rest	6–8 min jog, 3 min walk (x 3)	Rest	Rest/30 min walk	12–14 min jog, 3 min walk (x 2)
6	Rest/30 min walk	6–8 min jog (with bursts), 3 min walk (x 3)	Rest	2 min run, 3 min walk (x 5)	Rest	Rest/40 min walk	15–20 min jog without stopping
7	Rest/30 min cross-train	8–10 min jog (with bursts), 3 min walk (x 3)	Rest	2 min run, 3 min walk (x 6)	Rest	Rest/30 min cross-train	20–25 min jog (walk if needed)
8	Rest	10–12 min jog (with bursts), 3 min walk (x 3)	Rest	2 min run, 2 min walk (x 5)	Rest	Rest/30 min cross-train	25–30 min jog (walk if needed)
9	Rest/30 min cross-train	12–14 min jog (with bursts), 2 min walk (x 2)	Rest	2 min run, 2 min walk (x 6)	Rest	Rest/30 min cross-train	30–35 min jog (walk if needed)
10	Rest	15 min jog (with bursts), 2 min walk (x 2)	Rest	2–3 min run, 2–3 min walk (x 5)	Rest	Rest/40 min walk	35–40 min jog (walk if needed)
11	Rest	15 min jog (with bursts), 1–2 min walk (x 2)	Rest	2–3 min run, 2–3 min walk (x 6)	Rest	Rest/40 min walk	40–45 min jog (walk if needed)
12	Rest	15–20 min jog	Rest	20 min cross-train/rest	Rest	Rest/20 min walk	RACE DAY

Training plan 3: Novice 10k

WEEK	DAY 1	DAY 2	DAY 3	DAY 4	DAY 5	DAY 6	DAY 7
1	Gentle 10–15 min jog/walk	15–20 min jog	Rest	15–20 min jog (with bursts)	Rest/20 min cross-train	Rest	25–30 min, 3–4k jog
2	Rest	20 min jog	Rest	20 min jog (with bursts)	Rest/20 min cross-train	Rest	30–35 min, 4k jog
3	Rest	20–25 min jog	Rest	20–25 min jog (with bursts)	Rest/25 min cross-train	Rest	30–35 min, 4k jog
4	Rest	25 min jog	Rest	25 min jog (with bursts)	Rest/25 min cross-train	Rest	35–40 min, 4–5k jog
5	Rest	25–30 min jog	Rest	25–30 min jog (with bursts)	Rest/30 min cross-train	Rest	40–50 min, 5–6k jog
6	Rest	30–35 min jog	Rest	30–35 min jog (with bursts)	Rest/30 min cross-train	Rest	50–60 min, 5–6k jog
7	Rest	35–40 min jog	Rest	4 min run, 4 min walk (x 4)	Rest/30–35 min cross-train	Rest	60–65 min, 6–7k jog
8	Rest	35–40 min jog	Rest	4 min run, 4 min walk (x 5)	Rest/35–40 min cross-train	Rest	70–75 min, 7–8k jog
9	Rest	40–45 min jog	Rest	4 min run, 3 min walk (x 4)	Rest/40 min cross-train	Rest	75–80 min, 8–9k jog
10	Rest	45 min jog	Rest	4 min run, 3 min walk (x 5)	Rest/40–45 min cross-train	Rest	80–90 min, 9–10k jog
11	Rest	50 min jog	Rest	4 min run, 3 min walk (x 6)	Rest/45–50 min cross-train	Rest	80–90 min, 9–10k jog
12	Rest	20–30 min gentle jog	Rest	10–15 min gentle jog	Rest/20 min cross-train	Rest	RACE DAY

'Fast-track 5k' plan

Whether it just took you ages to get around to signing up for an event, you have taken on a bet from a friend that you 'don't have it in you' to run a 5k, or if life has just been too hectic for you to start training, this six-week timetable is designed to get you in as good a shape as possible in a relatively short space of time.

It is far from ideal, as you are more likely to pick up injuries, but sometimes through no fault of your own you might find yourself in this predicament and a fast-track training plan is the only hope you have to got you through. It may not necessarily be sufficient to get you round the 5k without stopping, but it'll certainly get you in good enough shape to enjoy the day and run the vast majority of it.

As with all the other plans, everyone has very different levels of fitness and some people adapt to training far quicker than others, so feel free to add a session or drop a session depending on the time you have available. Although the closer you stick to this plan the more prepared you will be to tackle a 5k, it still falls short of being ideal preparation.

If you are hell bent on running the whole 5k come the day of the race and you hope this plan will help you achieve it, I'm afraid it won't unless you 'tweak' it a fair bit by adding an extra session every week and following the tips outlined below. If you discover you're a natural runner and find the plan too easy, I suggest you dip into the other 5k plans and integrate some of those sessions into your weekly training.

However, if you find the going tough, don't worry. Just do what you can and focus on gaining maximum enjoyment out of the training – there's always next year. Always listen to your body and, if you pick up a muscle or joint twinge, stop training and treat the injury before it gets worse.

The best advice I can give is not worry if you are not very fit – I certainly wasn't when I started training for the Bath Race for Life. If you are starting from scratch then build up your running distance slowly.'

Sandie Hillier

Training plan 4: Fast-track 5k

WEEK	DAY 1	DAY 2	DAY 3	DAY 4	DAY 5	DAY 6	DAY 7
1	Rest	5 min jog, 3–4 min walk (x 3)	Rest	5 min jog, 4 min walk (x 3)	Rest/30 min brisk walk	Rest	8–10 min jog, 4–5 min walk (x 3)
2	Rest	6 min jog, 3–4 min walk (x 3)	Rest	6 min jog, 4 min walk (x 3)	Rest/30 min brisk walk	Rest	10–14 min jog, 4–5 min walk (x 3)
3	Rest	7 min jog, 3–4 min walk (x 4)	Rest	7 min jog, 4 min walk (x 4)	Rest/35 min brisk walk	Rest	14–18 min jog, 4–5 min walk (x 3)
4	Rest	8 min jog, 2–3 min walk (x 4)	Rest	7 min jog, 3 min walk (x 4)	Rest/40 min brisk walk	Rest	18–22 min jog, 4–5 min walk (x 2)
5	Rest	9 min jog, 2–3 min walk (x 4)	Rest	9–10 min jog, 2 min walk (x 4)	Rest/45 min brisk walk	Rest	22–25 min jog, 4–5 min walk (x 2)
6	Rest	10 min jog, 2–3 min walk (x 4)	Rest	10 min jog, 2 min walk (x 3)	Rest	Rest	RACE DAY

Key points about the 'Fast-track 5k' plan

- Although this training timetable may sound more attractive to follow than the 10–12-week plan, it is far from perfect and you ideally need to spend longer than this preparing for a 5k race. The shorter your training plan, the more injury beckons, so bear this in mind.

- If your fitness levels are already pretty good, you might benefit from incorporating a session from the 'Personal best' plan (see pages 52–3).

Provided that you feel OK, there is no harm in increasing the intensity of a session if your body is willing and able.

- If you feel fit enough to make the sessions a bit tougher, why not try one or two of the following?
  - Add an extra session in the week.
  - Run an extra interval or two.
  - Run each interval a little faster.
  - Run a little further than indicated.
  - Reduce the walking times in between jogging intervals.

'Personal best' plans

No matter how fast you intend to run your 5k or 10k race, these plans have been designed to push you that much harder than the novice plans.

If you are determined to either beat a friend over the line or improve your previous best time, these timetables are ideal. Although they can be tweaked slightly to fit in around your work and family schedule, unlike the novice plans, there is not a great deal of compromise in terms of the intensity or regularity of these training plans. If you try to stick to the training schedules as closely as possible, you will reap the rewards of earning bragging rights over your friend or have the satisfaction of earning a new PB.

'Rather than spending money we didn't have on posh GPS devices, we found it just as easy to drive a certain route and measure how far it was. That way we knew how far our training runs were.'

'We also discovered early on that finding certain markers on the route, such as certain buildings, lamp posts and even the local chip shop, helped as an incentive to keep going.'

Katy Norris and Gemma Stainsby

Key points about the 'Personal best' plans

- Some of these sessions are pretty tough on the legs and lungs, so get yourself ready for some testing training sessions.

- The interval sessions are incredibly effective at improving your running speed and running efficiency, but make sure you don't push yourself too hard or run these hard sessions too regularly.

- You know you are running at the right speed for each interval when you find the last 30 seconds pretty tough going. If you are not breathing heavily after each interval – you aren't running fast enough.

- If your legs feel heavy or too tired to run a scheduled intense training run, it's OK to substitute it for a gentle jog instead – sometimes a rest is just as good for you if your body is asking for it.

Training plan 5: Personal best 5k

WEEK	DAY 1	DAY 2	DAY 3	DAY 4	DAY 5	DAY 6	DAY 7
1	Rest	15–20 min jog	Rest	15–20 min jog (with bursts)	Rest/20 min cross-train	Rest	20–25 min jog
2	Rest	20 min jog	Rest	15–20 min jog (with bursts)	Rest/20 min cross-train	Rest	20–25 min jog
3	Rest	20 min jog (with bursts)	Rest	20–25 min jog (with bursts)	Rest/20–25 min cross-train	Rest	30 min jog
4	Rest	5 min intervals × 4 (4–5 min rest)	Rest	15–20 min run	Rest/20–25 mins cross-train	Rest	30 min jog
5	Rest	5 min intervals × 4 (4–5 min rest)	Rest	15–20 min run	Rest/25–30 min cross-train	Rest	30–35 mins jog
6	Rest	5 min intervals × 5 (3–4 min rest)	Rest	20 min run	Rest/30–35 min cross-train	Rest	30–35 mins jog (with bursts)
7	Rest	3 min intervals × 6 (3–4 min rest)	Rest	20–25 min run	Rest/30–35 min cross-train	Rest	30–35 mins jog (with bursts)
8	Rest	3 min intervals × 7 (3–4 min rest)	Rest	20–25 min run	Rest/35–40 min cross-train	Rest	25–30 min run
9	Rest	2 min intervals × 8 (2–3 min rest)	Rest	25–30 min run	Rest/40 min cross-train	Rest	30 min run
10	Rest	2 min intervals × 10 (2–3 min rest)	Rest	15–20 min run/ Rest	Rest/20 min cross-train	Rest	RACE DAY

Training plan 6: Personal best 10k

WEEK	DAY 1	DAY 2	DAY 3	DAY 4	DAY 5	DAY 6	DAY 7
1	Rest	15–20 min 2–3k jog	Rest	20 min 3k jog (with bursts)	Rest/30 min cross-train	Rest	20–25 min 3–4k jog
2	Rest	20 min 3k jog (with bursts)	Rest	20 min 3k jog (with bursts)	Rest/30 min cross-train	Rest	25 min 4k jog
3	Rest	20 min 3k jog (with bursts)	Rest	20–25 min 3–4k jog (with bursts)	Rest/30 min cross-train	Rest	25–30 min 4–5k jog
4	Rest	20–25 min 3–4k jog (with bursts)	Rest	3–4k run	Rest/35–40 min cross-train	Rest	30–35 min 5–6k jog
5	Rest	1k intervals × 4–5 (4–5 min rest)	Rest	4–5k run	Rest/35–40 min cross-train	Rest	35–40 min 6–7k jog
6	Rest	1k intervals × 5–6 (4–5 min rest)	Rest	5k run	Rest/40 min cross-train	Rest	40–45 min 7–8k jog
7	Rest	1k intervals × 6–7 (4–5 min rest)	Rest	6–7k jog	Rest/40–45 min cross-train	Rest	45–50 min 8–9k jog
8	Rest	3 min 800m intervals × 8–9 (3–4 min rest)	Rest	6–7k run	Rest/40–45 min cross-train	Rest	50–55 min 9–10k jog
9	Rest	3 min 800m intervals × 9–10 (3–4 min rest)	Rest	7–8k run	Rest/40–45 min cross-train	Rest	50–60 min 9–11k jog
10	Rest	3 min 800m intervals × 6 (3 min rest)	Rest	5k jog	Rest/40–45 min cross-train	Rest	RACE DAY

7 stretching to prevent injuries

If this is your first ever running event and you are totally confused about whether you actually need to bother stretching before a run, you certainly aren't alone. Nearly all novice runners find themselves doing a selection of random stretches before their first run, without really knowing which muscles they are stretching or whether they are stretching them properly. Over the years I have witnessed even accomplished runners performing the most bizarre, unnecessary and potentially dangerous back and leg stretches before a run, so I hope that this chapter will help you to stretch both effectively and safely.

A good stretching regime is essential before any form of physical exercise, for a number of reasons. Stretching is a vital part of preparing the muscles for physical exertion, it helps to keep them loose and, as a result, significantly reduces your chances of picking up annoying and often unnecessary injuries.

❖ side-stepping those nasty niggles

Recreational running has never been more popular despite having, over the years, earned a reputation as an activity that invites injury. Even the most dedicated of runners has been heard to say that there are two types of runner: 'those who are injured and those who are going to get injured'.

Running is repetitive and, as I mentioned earlier, during a run our feet and lower limbs have to tolerate the stress of the equivalent of three times our body weight with every stride. It's only natural to think that an injury is just waiting to happen.

However, before you give up on the idea of embarking on an activity that puts this much stress on your body, take comfort in the fact that our bodies have been designed to tolerate such stresses. There is no reason why you shouldn't be able to run for years without picking up an injury – provided that you look after your muscles and stretch them regularly.

By making sure all your major muscles and joints are well stretched you are guaranteed to not only walk (rather than hobble) to the start line on race day, but your whole training experience will be so much more enjoyable if you don't need to nurse sore knees, ankles and hips every week.

❖ stay balanced

Of all the analogies to demonstrate how important it is to keep your muscles strong and stretched,

picture a ship's mast with all the supporting guy ropes is perhaps the best way to illustrate the relationship between your muscles and your bones.

If you think of the mast as your spine, pelvis or one of your leg bones and the attached guy ropes as muscles, you'll see how important it is to keep them well stretched and strong, to prevent the 'mast' from being pulled and causing strain at the point where the ropes attach.

For runners, whose leg muscles often become tighter as their weekly miles creep up, it is vitally important to stretch regularly so that the major running muscles in the legs do not become excessively tight. If they do, they start to pull on the soft tissues around areas such as the pelvis or the knees, and cause pain and inflammation.

Equally important is to keep certain muscles strong, so that structures such as your pelvis are well supported with each running stride and the 'mast' can stay stable and prevent wobbling about during a run, which can ultimately lead to injuries.

Muscle balance and how it can prevent injuries is extremely complex and beyond the scope of this

book. So, to avoid confusion by using complicated terminology that would be better suited to a PhD sports science book, I have kept the following stretches and exercises simple – but they are still highly effective.

⁂ stretch, stretch, stretch

The need to stretch before and after exercise is actually quite a contentious issue among sports medicine experts, with some making the case that there is actually no need to stretch at all. Like so many scientific studies – such as debates on the evidence for anything from climate change to infant vaccinations – contradictory studies on the effectiveness of pre- and post-run stretching confuse so many people that they are often left with no idea of what is right and what is wrong.

Exception to the rule

As always, there is an exception to the rule when it comes to stretching.

If you are one of those people who are naturally very bendy and can't understand why other people find it so difficult to touch their toes, bend their fingers right back or hyper-extend their knees, then you really don't need to focus much time on stretching. Some people have a naturally high level of flexibility, and further stretching can actually be detrimental and cause joint instability. If this is you, then you are better off spending more time on the strengthening exercises in Chapter 7, to keep your joints strong and stable.

Having trained and prepared hundreds of people for various sporting events over the years, all with varying levels of flexibility, my stance is that, most of the time, stretching is an integral part of the warm-up and cool-down process of any form of exercise – especially running. When you consider the analogy of the ship's mast, it only stands to reason that the muscles should be well stretched before you attempt any form of physical activity. By ensuring the fibres in all the major leg muscles are well aligned, they are then able to contract smoothly and reduce any tension and potential injury that a tight muscle can cause.

pre-run stretching essentials

Before you flick forward a few pages and throw yourself into a series of stretches, there are three essential things you must remember when it comes to stretching. Although, by and large, stretching the

muscles before and after a run is a safe and effective procedure, it is so easy to take it for granted and do yourself damage if you fail to follow these golden stretching rules.

1. Always warm up the muscles

Warming up before any exercise is essential for a number of reasons: it lubricates the joints and raises core body temperature, but the primary purpose is to stimulate blood flow to the muscles, which both 'wakes them up' in preparation for exercise and also makes them easier to stretch.

Unfortunately, it is often the most conscientious runners that ignore this rule and who think they are being sensible by stretching before a run, when in actual fact they could be doing more harm than good. Placing a cold muscle in a stretch puts it under a great deal of strain as the fibres do not respond well unless they are warm. Your muscles react in a similar way to plasticine, which stretches easily when it's warm and breaks easily when it's cold.

To avoid straining a muscle before you've even got through the front door, try to make sure your leg muscles are nice and warm by either going for a gentle walk or jog for a good five minutes before you perform your stretches.

2. Stretch, don't strain

The key to effective stretching is to put the muscle you are trying to stretch in a stretched position, not a strained position. I've lost count of the number of times I have seen runners putting themselves through a torturous-looking stretching session with pained expressions on their faces, and pushing so hard that you fear their muscle is about to snap.

For every stretch illustrated on the following pages, push the muscle only to a point where you feel it is stretching, and then hold. After 20 seconds or so you will feel the stretch ease and then you can

push a little further – but please (especially men) do not see stretching as a competition and a way to prove to the next person that you are more flexible than them. It'll only end in a hamstring or groin tear and set your training schedule back a few weeks.

3. Take your time

Not only do individual levels of flexibility vary greatly, with one person barely able to touch their knees from a standing position and someone else easily able to kiss them, the ways our muscles respond to stretches also vary. Whereas one person might feel the stretch ease after 10 seconds, another person might need to hold it for a good 50 seconds, sometimes longer.

Because of this huge variation in stretch responses, always hold a stretch for as long as it takes for the muscle to ease before you either push it further, or change to stretch the other leg. It might take five seconds, it might take two minutes but, above all, don't rush your stretches. Take your time and start a training run only when your muscles feel good and ready.

post-run stretching essentials

Exhausted, in desperate need of a drink and with a hot shower calling your name, the post-run stretch is often ignored by runners, but if you can manage just a few minutes of light stretching after your jog, your muscles will thank you for it. Although it doesn't make a huge difference if you leave it until after your shower and drink, it's often a good idea to get it over and done with before you forget.

Although I'd be the first to admit that I've skipped the cool-down part of a run once in a while, it remains an important part of your training session, as a gentle walk can help reduce the symptoms of light-headedness and a drop in blood pressure that can occur if you stop suddenly after a tough run. Just as important as a gentle walk, however, is the post-run stretch.

Stretch preparation

With around 640 muscles in the human body, stretching every one of them before a run is not only impossible but also, quite obviously, a complete waste of time. As already mentioned, due to the variability in each runner's response to stretching some of you will have to spend more time than others stretching out the muscles before and after a run, but on average you should be looking to spend at least five minutes stretching out the key running muscles.

I recommend that you do the following stretches before and after every run. You could do more stretching, you could do less, but by stretching the muscles as outlined below, you will be well prepared to take on a training run, safe in the knowledge that all of your major running muscles are well stretched and ready to handle however many kilometres you want them to run.

about while at the same time paying the nursery bill, I suggest heading out the door as soon as you are dressed: cue up an inspirational running song on your MP3 player and set out for a brisk walk or gentle jog to get those muscles nice and warm.

If you're warming up outside, for your 5–10-minute warm-up, depending on your fitness level, try a combination of walking, power walking and very light jogging. Always start with a gentle walk and gradually increase the intensity until the end of the warm-up, where you should find yourself jogging lightly for a few minutes.

Having run hundreds of different types of routes over the years, and taken clients through their pre-stretch warm-ups, I've found that, whatever the route, there's always an ideal place to stop and stretch 5–10 minutes away from the front door. A tree, a park bench, a road sign or even a lamp-post are never far away, and they are all great places for you to stop and have a good stretch.

The warm-up

I cannot stress how important it is to warm up your muscles before you stretch.

The 'pre-stretch' warm-up should be an integral part of your training programme as it gets you into the right mindset and ready to tackle your training session. For this reason I always think it's best to spend the first 5–10 minutes of your training session warming up outside (jogging or walking), to get you well and truly in the mood.

Although it's perfectly OK to warm up, and even stretch, in the comfort of your home before you head out of the front door, I often find that it is so easy to get sidetracked by kids, the other half or even an overflowing laundry basket. Home warm-ups are a procrastinator's dream (and I speak from experience) as there are so many things that you can do (while stretching) to delay your training run. So, to prevent what should be a 5–10-minute warm-up turning into a 30-minute combination of swinging your legs

Bad weather

If the weather is really awful and the prospect of spending any longer outside than you need to is far from appealing, then you can warm up inside by:

- walking up and down the stairs a dozen or so times;
- performing some gentle leg swings while holding on to a chair;
- lying on your front and performing some gentle 'bum kicks' for a few minutes;
- doing a handful of gentle squats, making sure your knees do not come over the front of your feet (you should still be able to see your toes); achieve this by sticking your bum out while performing the squat, as if you are about to sit down in a chair.

Running the road

Be warned. If you stop and stretch near a busy road, expect the occasional honk of a car or truck horn – and, if you are 'lucky', a wolf whistle or two. It seems that runners attract a lot of attention from drivers, so don't be alarmed if you are urged to 'run faster' or you're complimented on the shape of your derriere. There's not a lot you can do about it, so either ignore it or respond in whatever way you deem appropriate!

The key stretches

The good news is that you will only really need to concentrate on stretching 14 key running muscles (seven on each leg). These are:

- the quadriceps (big muscle of the thigh);
- the hamstring (big muscle at the back of the leg);
- the calves (muscles at the back of the lower leg);
- the adductors (long muscles on the inside of your leg);
- the hip flexors (muscles that run in front of the pelvis);
- the gluteus maximus (your main 'bum muscle');
- the piriformis (your deep bum muscle).

There are dozens of variations of all these stretches, so feel free to use those presented here alongside others if you wish. The most important thing is to make sure you stretch all these key muscles before a run, as they are the ones that will be propelling you across the ground and are at the biggest risk of being damaged if they are not well stretched.

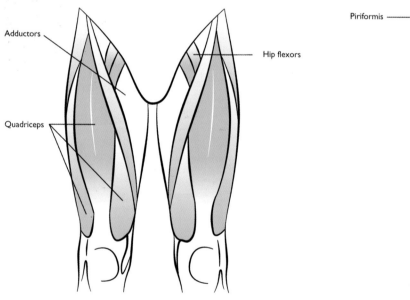

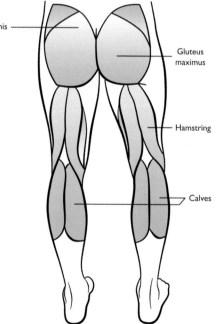

The quadriceps

The quads are probably the easiest muscles to stretch as this can be done in a number of different ways – standing up, kneeling down or lying down.

- Make sure you are steady while performing this stretch, so grab hold of a park bench, tree or wall. Falling over while stretching is pretty embarrassing (I know) so make sure you are well balanced.

- Standing nice and upright, reach behind you, take hold of one foot and slowly bring it towards your bum until you feel a stretching sensation down the front of your thighs.

- As some of you may be more flexible than others, it's perfectly possible that your foot could reach your bum without feeling any stretch. If this is the case, you can increase the stretch by slowly rotating your pelvis upwards.

- Hold the stretch for 15–20 seconds, then repeat with the other leg.

- Feel free to repeat the process two or three times, or until your quads feel stretched.

Quad stretch

'After training for a number of 5k and 10k events, I have found stretching after a run incredibly important. Since I started stretching religiously after every run, my back problems, which have plagued me for years, have been kept at bay. No matter what you do after a run, make sure you stretch.'

Sally May

The hamstrings

Behind your thighs lie the large hamstring muscles. Although these are important during a run, they are generally in 'cruise control' during long and steady-paced runs. They are used far more during explosive movements such as accelerating, so if you are the competitive type and looking to do some serious speed training then make sure your hamstrings are well stretched.

- If you are stretching near a low wall or park bench, you might find it easier to place your foot on it to raise your leg rather than keeping it on the floor (see Hamstring stretch 2).

Hamstring stretch

- With the leg you want to stretch extended in front of you, bend the supporting leg slightly and, if required, rest your hand gently on your thigh.

- Very slowly, lean your upper body forward, ensuring your back remains straight.

- After leaning 20 or so degrees, you'll feel a stretching sensation on the back of the extended leg.

- Hold the stretch for 15–20 seconds (or until you 'feel' the muscle become taut), then repeat with the other leg.

- Either way, always make sure your back is kept nice and straight during the entire stretch.

- Feel free to repeat the process two or three times, or until your hamstrings feel well stretched.

Hamstring stretch 2

Additional hamstring stretch

Although the stretch opposite is sufficient to stretch the hamstrings in preparation for a run, there is another more dynamic stretch you can do to really wake up the legs and excite the nervous system. This has the added advantage of waking up sleepy legs (making it perfect for morning runners) as well as raising the heart rate a few notches and really getting you ready to run.

- It is particularly important to hold on to a solid object for this stretch, so grab hold of something and make sure there is nothing directly in front of you or behind you.

- Standing nice and upright, slowly start to swing your leg in a pendulum-like motion. Start very slowly and gradually increase your leg's range of movement over the space of 30–40 seconds.

- By the end, you should be swinging the leg freely and it should have stretched well beyond its initial range of movement.

- Repeat this dynamic hamstring stretch a couple of times for each leg, and afterwards your legs will feel supercharged and ready to run.

Additional hamstring stretch

Additional hamstring stretch (continued)

The calves

Of all the leg muscles you need to look after and stretch, it is your calf muscles you should pay the most attention to. If you were to stretch only one muscle before a run, it should be your calves.

During a run, your calves are workhorses and are put under a lot of strain. If you fail to stretch them properly or regularly, you are putting yourself at risk of picking up a range of injuries, from Achilles tendonitis (see page 118) to rear knee pain.

This muscle is often very tight, especially in new runners and especially in women who wear heels a lot, so feel free to repeat the stretch a number of times both before and after your run, as well as throughout the day.

Expert corner

There are actually two calf muscles – gastrocnemius and the soleus.

Most calf stretches concentrate on stretching the gastrocnemius, which is the superficial calf muscle and the one which works the hardest out of the two during a running gait. However, the soleus muscle also works pretty hard and some runners may benefit from giving it a good stretch to help prevent it shortening and becoming susceptible to injury.

To stretch the soleus muscle, place your foot about six inches from a wall (with your toes pointing towards it) and slowly bend your knee. Try and make sure your heel remains on the floor and if your soleus is tight, you'll find that your deep calf muscle will get a stretching sensation the closer your knee gets to the wall. As always, hold the stretch for around 15 seconds and then swap legs.

- Find a solid object to place your hands on, which can be your trusty park bench, tree or wall, just so long as the object is immoveable.

- With your front leg bent, extend the other leg well behind you, keeping your heel placed on the ground.

- Slowly lean forwards, keeping your rear heel on the ground and your back leg straight. You should start to feel quite an intense stretch on the calf muscle of this back leg.

- Hold the stretch for 15–20 seconds, then repeat with the other leg.

- You can change the emphasis of the stretch by bringing the back leg in a foot or so and bending the leg at the knee – but remember to keep the heel on the ground.

Calf stretch

Additional calf stretch

As you progress through your training, you'll realise that your calves have this incredible ability to tighten up really easily and therefore need far more stretching than any other muscle. For this reason, I often suggest to runners that they stretch their calf muscles every day – even on 'days off'.

The best way to do this is either by performing the above stretch at home or at the office – or, even better, perform another calf stretch using a step.

- Find a step or stairs at home or at the office, and face 'upstairs'.

- Place the ball of one foot on the step and slowly drop your heel downwards; feel that lovely stretching sensation on your calf muscle.

- Hold the stretch for 15–20 seconds, then repeat with the other leg.

Useful tips

If you find that your muscles are particularly stubborn to stretch and need a helping hand, a foam roller may be just what you need.

Foam rollers are becoming increasing popular with runners to help relieve muscular tension in the ITB (side of the leg), piriformis, calf muscles and thighs through a process known as self myofascial release.

Although this sounds complicated, essentially all it means is that by using the foam roller you are able to deeply massage your muscles and encourage them to relax. Unfortunately, this process of rolling your tight muscles isn't the most pain free of experiences, but the benefits far outweigh the mild discomfort.

- As with the previous stretch, you can change the emphasis by bending your knee while keeping your heel dropped.

- Feel free to repeat this stretch several times a day, but always remember to be gradual and gentle with every stretching movement.

Additional calf stretch

The adductors

The adductor muscles are on the inside of your leg and play a key role in keeping you stabilised during running. Like your hamstrings, they are generally in 'cruise control' during a slow and steady run but are recruited far more the faster you run. For those of you who plan to use interval training as a key part of your weekly training regime, keep the adductors well stretched as groin injuries can be difficult to get rid of.

- Standing upright, face forwards and extend one leg to the side with your foot angled 45 degrees away from you. The other leg must remain straight and the foot pointing forwards.

Stretching tip

If your training regime involves mixing up your runs, such as sprint training one day and hill running a few days after, it is really important that you are particularly strict with your adductor stretches.

The adductors are highly effective stabilising muscles during a running gait at the best of times, but when they are worked extra hard during high intensity sessions such as hills and sprints, you need to stretch them extremely well, both before and after tough runs.

- Slowly shift your weight to the side of the bent leg and you will begin to feel a stretch on the inside of the straight leg.

- Make sure your hips are facing forwards at all times or you won't feel the maximum benefit of the stretch.

- Hold the stretch for 15–20 seconds, then repeat with the other leg.

Adductors stretch

The hip flexors

This group of muscles (made up of three separate muscles) is perhaps the most complicated area you have to stretch, as well as being one of the most important. Nearly on a par with the calf muscles, the hip flexor muscles are responsible for moving your thighs upwards, which as you can imagine makes them workhorses during a walk, jog or run.

Thankfully, the hip flexors are designed to tolerate a high workload, but at the same time it is essential that you keep them well stretched to prevent them shortening and causing a range of injuries, from back pain to muscle strain.

- Kneel down on the floor and extend one leg in front of you – bent at 90 degrees from the hip and 90 degrees from the knee.

Stretching tip

If, like many people, you experience low back pain, this stretch is an absolute must. This is because one of the main hip flexor muscles (called the psoas major) runs all the way from the top of your thigh bone to attach to the vertebrae in the lower back. If this muscle is not stretched and is shortened, not only by sitting down all day but also after a run, it can pull on the lower back and cause significant discomfort.

So, for the good of your back, it's a good idea to stretch the hip flexors every day and give yourself the best chance to be free from back pain, not only during and after your training, but possibly forever.

- From this position, slowly rotate your pelvis upwards. Imagine your pelvis is a bucket full of water and you're tipping a little bit of water out over your back side.

- The rotation of the pelvis alone might initiate a stretching sensation down the front of your rear leg but, if not, slowly move your whole body forwards until you feel a stretch.

- Hold the stretch for 15–20 seconds, then repeat on the other leg.

- You can perform an alternative, and slightly more effective, stretch if you assume a similar position but in a standing lunge position, with your back leg slightly bent.

Hip flexors stretch

Gluteus maximus

There are dozens of stretches for the large bum muscles, but this one is perhaps one of the easiest to perform and you can really feel the stretch working. It also has the added advantage of stretching the deep hip muscles.

As you can see, this stretch is not easy to do if you're out on the roadside, so it's perfectly OK to perform it before you head outside. Just make sure you stretch slowly and gently.

- Kneel down on the floor, and slowly lower your upper body to the ground assuming a press-up position, but resting on your forearms rather than your hands.

- Cross one knee over the other and slowly extend and straighten it backwards.

- As you straighten the leg, you'll notice that your bum slowly moves back and you'll start to feel a lovely stretch in the buttock.

- Hold the stretch for 15–20 seconds, then repeat on the other leg.

Stretching tip

The glute muscles are pretty awkward to stretch standing up and runners often feel a little self conscious trying to stretch them on the side of the road or by a park bench before they set off for a run. Therefore, there is no harm in giving it a good stretch in the comfort of your home before you head out of the front door. Make sure the muscle is warm by walking or jogging up the stairs a few times first and then perform a series of glute stretches before you go out for a run.

Gluteus maximus stretch

Additional gluteus maximus stretch

For those times when you're out on the road and it's not convenient to lie down and stretch out those all important butt muscles, this stretch is an excellent way to get them prepared for a run.

- Standing up straight, grab hold of an immoveable object such as a wall, tree or park bench.

- Keeping one leg firmly on the ground, with the knee soft, lift the opposite leg off the ground and pull the knee across the body.

- Try to make sure that your hips stay square during the stretch as this will maximise the stretch response.

- As you bring your knee up and across your body, you should feel the deep bum muscles of that leg start to stretch nicely.

- Hold the stretch for 15–20 seconds, drop that leg to the floor, then repeat on the other side.

Additional gluteus maximus stretch

'The biggest lesson I have learnt over my many years of recreational running is that if you are one of those people (like me), with tight and inflexible muscles you are almost certainly going to pick up an injury sooner or later if you don't take the time to stretch. The five or so minutes it takes to stretch out you main leg muscles before and after a jog is well worth doing – you'll only regret it if you don't.'

Ali Melvin

Piriformis stretch

The piriformis muscle is a deep bum muscle responsible for rotating the hip outwards. It is used mainly as a stabilising muscle during the running gait and can be the cause of quite significant pain if it is not stretched properly.

The piriformis is situated very close to the sciatic nerve, and if it becomes excessively tight it can put pressure on the nerve and give you, quite literally, a pain in the bum. Women in particular need to make sure this muscle is stretched regularly as they are particularly prone to compression in the sciatic nerve.

Piriformis stretch

- Lie on your back and bend both legs 90 degrees at the hips and knees.

- Place the ankle of the side you wish to stretch on the knee of the opposite leg.

- Grab hold of the leg you are not stretching and slowly pull it towards you.

- You will feel a stretch in the buttock of the other leg. Hold for 15–20 seconds and then change legs.

- When you feel the stretch, hold it for 15–20 seconds and slowly increase the stretch by leaning further forwards.

- Repeat on both sides until you feel looser.

Stretching tip

The piriformis is a really important muscle to keep well stretched, so if you find this stretch uncomfortable or difficult, do another stretch that you find easier. Dr Christopher Norris's book *Stretching for Running* is a great resource, and gives you a selection of stretches for the piriformis and other muscles. So if you find your muscles are tight and you need some extra help stretching, his book might just come in handy.

Case study

Name: Eileen Child

Age: 62

Occupation: Project Manager

Years of running experience: On and off for decades!

As my work is a half an hour drive away, computer driven and therefore chair bound I like to get my run over and done with early in the morning. This means that I am very careful to make sure that I have stretched fully after getting out of bed and before I start a run half an hour later.

My initial early routine covers things like ensuring that I have had plenty of water, and then stretching exercises. I always stretch out my spine first. So with fingers locked I fully extend my arms upwards trying to reach the ceiling while keeping my feet firmly on the ground. I then gently sway my body from side to side stretching left and right with fully extended arms.

To make sure that my leg muscles are stretched I manage about 10 lunges for each leg making sure I get as low as possible on each stretch forwards. I also then stretch out my calf muscles with one leg back and slightly bent with the other leg forward and stretching. Finally I stretch out the front thigh muscle by balancing on one foot and bending the other knee backwards and grabbing hold of my foot with the same side hand and pulling the foot upwards. I repeat these exercises for both legs. These are all the stretching routines I have learnt through fitness books and exercise classes.

I always start my run slowly to allow the muscles a chance to warm up properly. And if I still feel a need to stretch I will do a few more leg stretches before starting a jog. When the run is over, even if I am hot and tired, I spend a few minutes stretching out again usually using the same routine and this seems to prevent the aches and pain associated with the stiffness that can follow a run.

exercises to prevent injuries

Many of the 5k and 10k runners I spoke to during the research for this book said that along with stretching, they'd like to know what exercises to do to help with pre-existing injures such as sore knees and hips, and make running pain-free again.

I not only met dozens of runners who had themselves battled niggling injuries throughout their training, but also their friends and relatives who were cheering them on from the sidelines. Many of the spectators also desperately wanted to take part in the event, but were prevented from running due to an occurrence of a sore knee or hip, and were therefore forced to pull out.

Although the reasons why people develop sore joints from running vary hugely, most of the time joint pain can be both prevented and cured by a combination of stretching and strengthening of the key leg and core muscles, so hope is most certainly not lost if all this sounds familiar.

So, if you are a little nervous about whether your joints are up to the job of getting you around a 5k and 10k course, read on to see how there is every chance that you can fulfil your dream and take part in an event 'hobble free'.

This chapter highlights:

- which muscles are often to blame for causing sore joints;

- what exercises you can do to strengthen them;

- what exercises you can do to prevent common running injuries.

⁘waking sleepy muscles

Love it or hate it, as fun as modern life is, it also brings with it enforced long periods of inactivity. The office, the ease and availability of motorised transport and – if truth be told – our inherent laziness have led us to become a nation of 'couch potatoes' – a way of life that has helped to both expand our waistlines and deactivate a series of muscles whose job it is to keep us balanced and supported.

For wannabe runners, this problem of an inactive lifestyle means that many of the muscles that help us to run, and that help stabilise our body when we run, go to sleep and become inactive and weak. This weakness, although not immediately obvious, is the reason why so many runners pick up injuries and fail to gain maximum enjoyment from their training and the event they have entered.

We will look now at a few examples of common weak muscles.

The core muscles

The word 'core' is a bit of a buzz word in the world of fitness, and there is still much confusion about what exactly 'the core' is and what exactly it does to help the body to function properly.

Going into detail about the core and how it affects the moving body is a bit too technical for this book, but the following is a summary of what you need to understand about it as someone in training for a running event.

In essence, the core muscles of the body help to keep the trunk (mid-section) stabilised during a run, and are vital in supporting and protecting the spine and pelvis, acting a bit like a corset. It is estimated that over 90 per cent of people have 'sleepy' deep core muscles as a result of inactivity, and a lack of specific exercise exposes the body to a range of injuries from back pain to hip pain. However, the good news is that just a small selection of simple exercises can wake up the deep core muscles and prevent you from picking up injuries.

The glutes (your bum)

It's probably not something you're told every day, but the backsides of many people are not nearly as awake as they should be. The large muscles in your bum have a tendency to go to sleep if they are not exercised properly or regularly, which can have serious consequences for the stability of your pelvis and the health of your lower back.

The muscles in your butt are so important in providing stability for your pelvic region that if they are sleepy as a result of you sitting in the car or on a chair all day in the office, the support they give your pelvis is severely reduced – not a great situation if you are about to start training for a 5k or 10k run.

In addition, keeping your butt muscles strong and active is vital in both treating and preventing low back pain. So, for anyone who is a little anxious about how their back will stand up to the rigours of regular running, a few butt exercises are essential to keep your back happy.

☆train for gain – not pain

Now that you have some idea why you should do specific exercises in addition to your running, take a look at the following series of exercises and choose a selection that you think will help you with your training and assist in curing any pre-existing condition you might have. They might not work miracles for all conditions, but all of the following exercises have been chosen for this book as they have a proven track record in helping runners overcome annoying and often unnecessary injuries.

For most of the following exercises, you are given two options.

Fitting it all in

Unless you are lucky enough to have all the time in the world available to prepare for your race, the notion of adding these exercises to your already packed training week might seem like asking the impossible. However, these specific exercises have been given to you in the knowledge that time is tight, and you'll see that every one of these exercises can be done in the comfort of your living room and in front of the TV.

So why not kill two birds with one stone and get your *Corrie* or *EastEnders* fix at the same time as strengthening your core and buttocks?

1 Always start with exercise 1, which will get you used to the movement and will gently strengthen the muscles.

2 After a week or so, once you feel you are comfortable with the exercise and are getting stronger, you can progress on to exercise 2, which is a tad more intense and a little more challenging.

If you experience any significant joint pain while performing one of these exercises, stop immediately and leave that exercise alone. There are numerous reasons why some exercises might exacerbate certain previous injuries, so if you find yourself in discomfort, resist the temptation to soldier on.

Have a ball

To make life easy for those of you who either don't have a gym membership, don't want to have a gym membership or simply don't have the time to go to the gym as well as run, most of the following exercises can be performed without any equipment. For those exercises that suggest using something to assist with

them, you will easily be able to find something around the house to substitute anything you'd find in a gym.

However, if you are looking to buy a piece of fitness equipment to help out with the strengthening exercises in this chapter, I strongly recommend you look no further than an exercise ball.

Since its inception in the early 1990s, the fit ball/ Swiss ball/exercise ball (they all mean the same thing) has shown itself to be one of the most versatile pieces of equipment you can buy and, when you consider that you can pick one up for around £10 in Argos, they are a very worthwhile investment. Knowing which size ball to buy is difficult if you have never used one, but for the vast majority of people a ball measuring 55cm in diameter is ideal. If in doubt, choose a small ball over a large one.

Just some of the benefits include:

- Improved flexibility
- Improved core strength
- Improved overall body strength
- Balance training
- Spinal mobilisation (improved spine flexibility)

For a selection of the following exercises, I have included an extra exercise for those of you 'with balls', but remember that they are not essential – all the exercises can be performed easily on their own and without any equipment.

Work that booty

The bridge

There a number of different ways you can perform this exercise, both at home or in the gym, and it is one of the best ways to firm up those bum muscles and wake them up to help stabilise the pelvis and prevent you from getting injured.

Bridge 1

- Lie on your back with your legs bent at the knee and your feet flat on the floor.
- Place a cushion or ball the size of a small football in between your knees and squeeze gently.
- Keeping your feet flat on the floor slowly raise your bum off the ground about 6–8 inches and hold for a few seconds.

Bridge 1

- Slowly drop your bum back to the floor again, keeping that cushion/ball gently squeezed.
- Perform 15 'bum raises' three times, with a minute's rest in between sets.

Bridge 2

- Assume the same position as for Bridge 1, lying on your back with your legs bent at the knee and your feet flat on the floor.
- Place a cushion or ball the size of a small football in between your knees and squeeze gently.
- This time, extend one leg until it is straight, so that you have only one foot on the floor, with the other leg extended in the air.
- Make sure you keep squeezing the pillow/ball gently, and aim to keep your pelvis nice and square. This helps to really target the bum muscles and teach the body to enhance pelvic stability.
- Perform 15 'bum raises' three times on each leg, alternating legs.

Bridge 2

Strengthening tip

If you have mastered the Bridge 2 exercise and think you need an extra challenge to really tax those butt muscles, then try progressing by using the stability ball to rest your feet on. Follow the instructions for the Bridge 1 exercise, but instead of placing your feet on the floor, place them on the ball instead. The instability of the ball under your feet offers a really taxing workout out for those glutes and is the perfect progression from the Bridge 1 and 2 exercises. For an even tougher challenge, perform the Bridge 2 exercise, but with one foot on the ball.

Bridge on the ball

- Lie on the ball with your head and neck supported, your hips parallel to the floor, feet hip width apart and your hands resting on your waist.

- Keeping the ball still, lower your bum towards the ground 6–8 inches and then raise it back up again.

- Make sure your feet stay firmly on the floor and that you push through your heels as you lower and raise your bum – this ensures that your bum muscles are recruited effectively.

- Perform 15 movements three times.

- To make this even tougher, you can either narrow your stance so that your feet are touching, perform the movement on one leg, or even perform the exercise lying on the floor with your feet on the ball.

Bridge on the ball

Squats

Squats are a fantastic overall leg exercise and are particularly good at strengthening the bum and thigh muscles. They can be done anywhere and made as hard as you like – if you enjoy making life difficult for yourself.

Squat 1

- Stand upright, facing forwards with your feet hip width apart.
- Slowly lower your bum towards the floor as though you are trying to sit on a chair.
- As you squat, make sure your knees do not come over the front of your feet and stay over your ankles (you should still be able to see your toes).
- Squat to at least 45 degrees (no lower than 90) and come back up again, pushing through your heels as you do so.
- Try to make sure you keep the body upright throughout the movement and remember to push your bum back.
- Perform 15 repetitions three times, with a 2–3 minute break between sets.

Squat 1

Squat 2

- Find something you can hold on to, such as a wall or a door.
- Assume the same position as for Squat 1, but this time raise one leg off the ground.
- Making sure you are well balanced, slowly begin a squat movement making sure your knee does not come over the front of your foot and your back stays straight.
- As this exercise is much more difficult than Squat 1, you will find it almost impossible to squat as low, so start off cautiously and lower only when you feel comfortable.
- Perform 10–15 repetitions three times, with a 2–3 minute break between sets.

Squat 2

Squat tip

To make sure your knees are in the correct position when you perform a squat you should try to make sure that, as you progress through the movement, the centre of your knee tracks through your second toe (the one next to your big one).

Ball squat

The benefits of performing a squat with the ball are that it helps to keep the back straight and makes it far easier to perform the squat correctly and effectively.

- Find a solid wall and place the ball in the small of your back, so that it feels comfortable.

- Assume the same position as with normal squats with your feet hip width apart, but instead of standing up completely straight, stand with your legs slightly further in front of you.

- Using the ball as a support, slowly squat down no lower than 90 degrees, again making sure that your knees do not come forwards over your toes. If they do, simply move your feet slightly further forwards.

- Make sure you push through your heels to make the bum work extra hard. Enjoy!

- Perform 15 repetitions three times, with a 2–3 minute break between sets.

Ball squat

Prone thigh raises

These exercises are little gems as they not only really target the bum muscles but have the added benefit of helping to strengthen the lower back as well.

Note: during these exercises, you will feel your lower back muscles working, which may be a little uncomfortable – if you feel pain, however, stop immediately.

Thigh raise 1

- Lie flat on your front, with your head resting on your hands.

- Bend one leg at the knee at 90 degrees, while keeping the other one still and straight.

- Without lifting any part of your pelvis off the ground, slowly raise the thigh of your bent leg off the ground a few inches, hold for a second or two, and then lower it back down.

- Perform 15–20 repetitions three times.

- To save time, why not alternate legs so that, once you have performed 15–20 raises on one leg, swap to the other one straight away?

Thigh raise 1

Thigh raise 2 – on the ball

Using the ball for a thigh raise exercise is far more intense than doing it on the floor, so do be careful when first trying it. If you feel any pain in your lower back, stop immediately.

- Lie face down on the ball so that your lower stomach is positioned in the middle of it.

- With your working leg bent at the knee and the other straight, rest on your hands to stop you from rolling forwards. Raise your thigh off the ball just above horizontal, hold for a second or two, and slowly drop it back down again.

- Perform 15–20 repetitions on each leg three times.

- Feel free to add variety, by alternating legs after each repetition. This helps to challenge your core as well as your bum muscles.

Thigh raise 2 – on the ball

Core exercises

Abdominal hollowing

Also known as the 'four-point tummy vacuum test' this exercise is key to waking up your sleepy deep stomach muscles and making them actively protect your back during your running training. Although this exercise is best performed on your hands and knees, it can actually be done in any position at any time of the day, from standing up cooking dinner to driving to work. It is quite tricky to master, but once you've got it there will be no stopping you.

Abdominal hollowing 1

- Assume a kneeling position, with your hands placed directly below your shoulders and your knees directly below your hips.

- It is essential that you keep your back straight so that if you placed a pole on your back it would lie parallel to the floor and touch the back of your head, your upper back and your bum.

- Take a deep breath in and let your stomach drop towards the floor.

- Keeping your back straight, breathe out, draw your belly button towards your spine and hold.

Abdominal hollowing 1

- Keep your stomach sucked in for as long as you can before taking a breath and repeating the procedure.

- Perform 10–15 'stomach sucks' two or three times with a 2–3 minute break between sets.

Abdominal hollowing 2

Once you have you got to grips with how to hollow your stomach effectively, you are ready to move on to this exercise. It is also known as the 'horse stance' and is a lot harder than many people think: it might look like a piece of cake, but to do it well is difficult, so take your time and it will really help to strengthen your core and protect your back during your training.

- Assume the same positions as you did for Abdominal hollowing 1, making sure your back remains straight throughout the exercise.

- Take a deep breath in and let your stomach drop towards the floor.

- Keeping your back straight, breathe out and draw your belly button towards your spine; keep it in for

the duration of the exercise, while breathing normally.

- When ready, lift one hand and the opposite knee off the floor a tiny bit – less than half a centimetre.

- Hold for 10 seconds, then repeat on the other side.

- Perform 10 repetitions two or three times, with a 2–3 minute break between sets.

Abdominal hollowing 2

If at first you don't succeed ...

The process of sucking your stomach in while breathing out can feel very odd to start with, and completely the opposite of what you feel is normal. Most people find it more natural to suck their tummies in when they breathe in and trying to do the opposite is like trying to pat your head and rub your stomach at the same time. It is tough, but persevere and you will get there.

Stretching tip

If you are new to the concept of abdominal hollowing it can be quite tricky to master, often leaving you in doubt as to whether you are doing it properly. The best position to get to grips with hollowing your stomach is often on all fours. Although, once mastered, it can easily be performed standing up, sitting down, standing on your head, when you are starting out, most people find it far easier to execute on their hands and knees.

Lower abdominals

There are several schools of thought when it comes to the lower abdominals, with some experts claiming that there is no such thing as 'lower' stomach muscles and that all abdominal musculature is the same.

Personally, I believe they very much do exist and, if they are untrained and weak, this can lead to quite severe pelvic instability due to your body being unable to coordinate leg movement while at the same time keeping the pelvis stable. This can cause a range of issues, especially low back pain.

Lower abdominals 1

- Lie flat on your back with your knees bent at 90 degrees and your feet flat on the floor.

- Place one or two hands in the small of your back and draw your stomach in the same way as you did for the Abdominal hollowing exercises.

- Slowly tilt your pelvis so that you apply pressure to your hands – not so hard that you cut off the blood supply.

- Hold this pressure for around 10 seconds and relax.

- Repeat the exercise 10 times with a 2–3 minute break between sets.

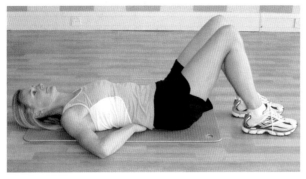

Lower abdominals 1

Lower abdominals 2

- Assume exactly the same position as for Lower abdominals 1.

- With your hands compressed in the small of your back and your tummy hollowed, slowly slide your feet away from your body, without releasing the pressure on your hands.

- Start by sliding your feet away just a few inches; as you get stronger you'll be able to straighten them further.

- Hold each position for 10 seconds and repeat three times, with a 2–3 minute break between sets.

Lower abdominals 2

Don't give up

To the casual onlooker, it will look like you are hardly doing anything but many people find abdominal exercises incredibly tough. When doing abdominal hollowing exercises, as soon as you rotate your pelvis and squash your hand you'll feel your lower stomach muscles firm up and really start to work to keep your pelvis stable – don't be surprised if you feel your stomach start to shake.

Lateral double leg raise

This exercise is another one of those that looks easy but is actually pretty hard to do. The side double leg raise is an excellent exercise to help strengthen the muscles on the side of your stomach, which help to support the trunk during your running training. It also has the added benefit of helping to keep those glutes nice and strong.

Double leg raise 1

- Lie on your side, on a soft surface such as a carpet or mat, with your head resting on your arm and your legs kept nice and straight.

- Keeping perfectly side on and your pelvis nice and stable, slowly raise both legs off the ground an inch or two and hold for a few seconds.

- Slowly lower your legs back down to the floor and repeat 10 times.

- Perform 10 repetitions three times on each side with a 2–3 minute break between sets.

Double leg raise 1

Double leg raise 2

- Assume the same position as for Double leg raise 1.

- Instead of raising both legs off the ground to the same height, this time lift both legs up a few inches then let the top leg move up a few more inches.

- Keeping the pelvis and upper body still, move your legs towards each other in a 'scissor' movement.

- Perform 10 'scissors snips' then repeat on the other side.

- Repeat the exercises three times on each side with a 2–3 minute break in between sets.

Double leg raise 2

Double leg raise tip

Keeping your body still during this exercise can be tough, especially when your legs are moving, so feel free to place your top hand on the floor to stop you from wobbling about. As you get stronger, you'll find that your stability will improve and you won't need to rely on that hand to stop you from toppling over.

Stomach strengtheners

There are literally dozens of exercises you can do to strengthen your stomach muscles, so to save you the confusion of trying to guess which ones are best for your running training, I have hand picked my top two.

Although the following stomach exercises are illustrated without any equipment, they can also be done using an exercise ball by placing your feet on the ball. The instability of the ball taxes your core muscles far more intensely.

Stomach strengthener 1

- Assume the press-up position, with your hands shoulder width apart.

- Maintaining perfect alignment of your spine, so that the back of your head, upper back and bum are in a straight line, hold the position for as long as you can.

- Once you feel your back dip or your stomach finds the going too tough, stop, have a break for 2–3 minutes and repeat the exercise.

Stomach strengthener 1

Stomach strengthener 2

- Assume exactly the same position as for Stomach strengthener 1, but instead of placing your hands shoulder width apart, bring them closer together so that you form a triangle shape with your thumbs and forefingers.

- Make sure you keep perfect alignment of your spine, so that the back of your head, upper back and bum are in a straight line; hold the position for as long as you can.

- Once you feel your back dip or your stomach finds the going too tough, stop, have a break for 2–3 minutes and repeat the exercise.

- Perform 5 to 10 times.

Stomach strengthener 2

Although these stomach strengthening exercises are ones you may not be familiar with, while they are excellent, there is no reason why you can't perform some more conventional stomach exercises in conjunction with them. Good old fashioned abdominal crunches, which most people have done in a gym class or two over the years, are still highly effective at strengthening the stomach muscles and can also help to prevent nasty side stitches. If you are unsure how to perform them correctly, always consult a fitness professional and seek their advice. If there is one thing worse than not paying attention to strengthening your stomach muscles, it's performing stomach exercises incorrectly.

Stretching tip

If you have excessively tight thigh or hip flexor muscles, you may find that you will not be able to lift your leg very high off the ground. If this is the case, always make sure that you stretch these muscles very well before attempting the exercise.

It's also worth knowing that the thigh raiser exercises can also be performed with the working leg straight as well as bent. Always make sure you are in full control of the movement and never rush it – the more controlled you move the leg and the more stable you keep your pelvis the better.

9

go-faster fuel

Irrespective of how well your training goes, backing it up with good-quality nutrition is essential if you are to get the most out of your preparations and race day itself.

❖ you are what you eat

When it comes to training for any event, be it a 5k jog or a full marathon, many runners forget about the importance of eating well and instead spend most of their time focusing on their training programme and clocking up the kilometres.

As well as concentrating on the physical aspect of training, it is also really important to pay close attention to your diet. Good-quality nutrition is essential in everyday life, let alone when you are making your body cover dozens of kilometres every week, so make a conscious effort to follow the guidelines in this chapter and feed yourself the right fuel to give you all the energy your need. After all, you are what you eat!

By following just a few simple dietary guidelines you can directly influence your energy levels; this will help you to train week in week out, and will give you the oomph required to get the most out of those hard-working legs.

A few food facts to digest

The difficult thing about eating the right food is that often some of the things we think are healthy are in fact either bursting with hidden fats and/or salt, or contain vast quantities of hidden sugar. This is bad enough for you when you are leading a sedentary lifestyle, but when you eat poor-quality foods when you're in training for a running event, it can have a serious impact on how you feel.

To give you an idea of some of the hidden nasties out there, here are a few obvious ones, plus some that might surprise you.

- A single Big Mac contains approximately 490 calories – to expend that much energy, you'd need to run just under five miles.
- A Starbucks grande Caffè Latte contains 223 calories – this will take just over 2 miles, or 20 minutes, of running to burn off.
- A small (175ml) glass of wine contains approximately 150kcals – so just two glasses in the evening will take you about three miles of running to burn off.
- Even a couple of 'healthy eating' sausages can contain up to a third of your recommended daily allowance of salt.

⁖burning those calories

It goes without saying that, over the course of your training, you are going to be expending far more calories every day that you did before you began your race preparations.

Every day? Yes, every day. Even on rest days.

This often confuses people new to running (or even power walking), but it's a fact that when you start exercising regularly, your body's metabolism is elevated as it works to help the body adapt to the increased workload you are placing on it.

After you've finished a run, your metabolic rate is increased significantly for the first 2 hours and remains slightly elevated for up to 24–48 hours, depending on how hard or how fast you have run. So although it might sound too good to be true, the day after a tough training run you will still be burning calories even while at rest – making you feel a little less guilty if you accidentally find yourself raiding the biscuit barrel.

Initially, especially for very new runners, you may not notice any difference in your metabolism but, after a few weeks, don't be surprised if you:

- feel a lot warmer while 'at rest' than you did before training;

Metabolism explained

Put simply, your metabolism, or metabolic rate, is the term used to describe the process by which the body converts the food you eat into energy to help the body work at an optimal level. If you delve deep into the subject of metabolism, you'll come across terms such as 'basal metabolic rate' and 'resting metabolic rate', but to save unnecessary confusion, just think of it as the amount of energy your body needs to perform all your physiological functions – from breathing, to thinking, to kidney function. All your organs require a certain amount of energy in order to work at their best and, when you start training, the extra stimulation of your muscles increases your body's metabolic rate.

- feel a little more peckish at random times of the day;
- feel a lot more energetic and full of beans.

The feeling of a raised metabolism as a result of training can be fantastic, and with the added bonus that this elevation in metabolism is helping your body to melt away unwanted fat, it makes the tough training sessions in the pouring rain all the more worthwhile.

How much energy?

Knowing how much energy you are going to need to fuel your training sessions is not an easy question to answer as everyone has very different energy requirements. Due to variations in runners' muscle mass, activity levels and genetics, everyone will have slightly different energy requirements, which makes it nearly impossible to give an exact figure.

Over the years, sports scientists have tried to come up with a range of formulae to give people an idea of what their individual resting metabolic rate is, but most of these have proved inaccurate. Estimates such as multiplying your weight in kilograms by 2 and then by 11 (for women) and by 2 and then by 12 (for men) are all very well, but unless you are a professional athlete, knowing this figure is largely irrelevant.

Expert corner

According to world-renowned exercise physiologists David Costill and Jack Wilmore, a 13-stone male running at a 6:23 min/km pace (or 9.4kph) will burn approx 14 calories a minute, and a 10-stone woman running at the same pace will burn approx 11 calories a minute.

As a first-time runner and someone who has entered a 5k or 10k race for a bit of fun, try not to get too obsessed with knowing the exact amount of energy you'll need to meet your training demands. Unlike your marathon-running counterparts, unless you follow a very poor diet or eat very little, your body is able to store more than enough energy to see you through even your longest and hardest training runs, and across the finish line on race day.

Besides, the important thing is not how much energy you consume, but what kind of energy you consume. In the same way that a diesel car won't go very far on a tank full of unleaded, your body, too, needs a certain type of fuel to keep it moving and able to tolerate the demands of your training regime. Put the wrong fuel in the tank and you could find the going gets tough before you've even started.

eating for energy

Over the course of your training, your body is going to convert what you eat into energy and use it to fuel every training run you do, from your very first slow 10-minute power walk to your last 10k training run.

The trouble is, it is very easy to be fooled by your body as to the best types of food that will help you get the best out of your training. The body is so ingenious at adapting and making do with inadequate and poor-quality nutrients that it is sometimes difficult to know if what you are eating is actually the right thing for running training.

Unlike a car that will function only on one type of fuel, your body will do its best to convert whatever you eat into the nutrients it needs to make your heart beat, your brain think and your legs run. However, as much as this might sound like an invitation to take yourself off to KFC to fuel up for training, the body can only do so much with bad-quality ingredients. It may very well be able to use the nutrients from a fatty, salty chicken drumstick to fuel your next training run, but it will do so insufficiently and there is every chance that you'll feel lethargic and heavy legged for the duration of the session.

Do not underestimate the importance of eating well and taking on the right types of fuel. It might be possible to run after eating poor food, but the difference you'll feel if you eat properly will make you think twice about whether that greasy burger was actually worth it.

So, let's take a look at what you should be eating and, most importantly, why.

Carbohydrates

The word may put the fear of God into Atkins diet followers, but it is carbohydrate-rich foods that are ultimately responsible for providing you with the energy to train week in week out.

Without carbohydrates your legs will grind to a halt and the only place you'll be going is to the floor, as your blood sugar levels can sink too low and cause a range of symptoms, from light-headedness to disorientation. This is not the book to discuss the pros and cons of low-carbohydrate diets, but I strongly suggest that, if you are toying with the idea of following a low-carb diet, now is not the time. Every year, St John Ambulance volunteers are rushed off their feet with runners taken ill at races, a large proportion of whom are found to be suffering from low blood sugar, which most of the time can be avoided if you follow a sensible diet.

Which carbs to choose?

Carbohydrates are found in a wide range of foods in very different forms. From sugary snacks to wholegrain rice, the different types of carbohydrate that can be found on the shelves of the supermarket can be confusing, and it can be difficult to know

which type is the best to choose to help fuel your running training.

So, to help you out, the following summary of the different types of carbohydrate highlights those you should eat sparingly and those that should form part of your everyday diet.

Complex carbohydrates: your friends

Complex carbs are the type you should be eating every day to give you the energy to train. They provide the body with a steady stream of energy and help to keep you going through the day. The most popular choices are:

- Breads
- Rice } Brown is best as it contains more healthy fibre.
- Pasta
- Potatoes (baking, new or sweet – not chips!)
- Oats
- Cereals

All these options are fantastic for fuelling your body to give you the energy to run three or four times a week, but be careful not to overdo it. Just because you are training regularly, it doesn't mean that you need barrow loads of carbohydrate-rich foods to keep you going. The body is incredibly efficient at storing carbohydrate in the liver and muscles, ready to be called upon when needed, so provided that you eat sensible quantities of carbs every day, your reserves will be well stocked up.

Don't forget your veggies

For many people, the notion of replacing a meat-based meal with a vegetarian option may sound unappealing, but in the interests of your health, swapping a 'meat and two veg meal' with a vegetarian option once or twice a week is certainly worth considering.

Carb overload

Your muscles and liver are capable of storing approximately 500 grams of carbohydrate, which will provide you with enough energy to run up to 18 miles. This is usually the distance at which marathon runners hit the infamous 'wall' as the body has to rely on alternative energy sources to keep the legs moving.

For 5k and 10k events, provided you eat a well-balanced diet without going crazy and stuffing yourself with extra large bowls of spaghetti bolognaise, there is no reason why your carb levels should drop excessively.

Although this figure will vary hugely depending on gender, weight, fitness level and running speed, during a 5k or 10k race the amount of carbohydrate your body will use to fuel your run is anywhere between 125 grams and 225 grams, respectively. Even a 10k run at a fast pace will not even use up half of your body's internal carb stores, so think twice before piling on extra mash with your bangers.

Not only will a vegetarian dish help boost your fibre consumption and keep you regular, but the essential antioxidants and nutrients in different coloured vegetables play a major role in boosting immunity and warding off certain cancers.

Even if you are the most hardened of meat eaters, it's so easy to rustle up a tasty vegetarian meal and not feel short changed by the lack of meat on your plate. Just a few suggestions include:

- Roasting vegetables: Throw any vegetable you can think of into a deep baking tray, drizzle with olive oil and balsamic vinegar and throw it in the oven for 40 minutes. Garlic, onions, pumpkin, squash, broccoli and sweet potato make this dish an incredibly healthy and delicious meal, so why not experiment?

- Quorn: This is a massively underrated meat replacement and can be used in the same way as mince. Made from a range of vegetable proteins, quorn is a highly nutritious and tasty meat alternative that might surprise you.

- Stir-frying vegetables: This is another great way to give veggies maximum taste without leaving you pining for meat. Provided you use a variety of herbs, spices and oils you can make some really gutsy stir-fries purely with vegetables, so get in that kitchen and start experimenting.

Sugary carbs: the enemy

As tasty as they might be, sugary snacks should be avoided as much as possible. Although sugary foods such as biscuits, cakes and pastries are dense with carbohydrate, they contain the wrong type of carbs and are often also high in unnecessary fat.

The trouble with sugar is that it is very easily broken down by the body and ready to be used instantly as an energy source. As great as this might sound, this actually has the effect of raising your blood sugar levels too high and causing the body to secrete excessive amounts of insulin to try to store the sugar away in your muscles and liver. If the stores are already full, the sugar has nowhere to go and is instead stored as fat.

So, although it's unrealistic to expect you to completely steer away from sugary snacks for the duration of your training, try to keep them to a minimum. If temptation gets too much and you can't resist your favourite chocolate bar, save it for after a training run. This way, the sugar is far less likely to be stored away as fat and will instead be used to replenish the carbohydrate stores you have just burned off during your run.

Protein

Although protein-rich diets in sport are usually more synonymous with muscular sports such as rugby, boxing and weight lifting, runners also need to eat good-quality protein to help them through the tough weeks of training.

Protein has a number of different roles in the body, but for runners it is particularly valuable in terms of the nutrients needed to help your leg muscles recover from training runs. A diet containing insufficient amounts of protein, or poor-quality protein, will severely restrict the body's ability to repair itself after training, not only making future training runs a bit harder but also leaving you far more vulnerable to injury.

Remember, the body is remarkable at making do with whatever we eat and using it to keep the body functioning, but if your diet contains inadequate or insufficient protein, the body has little choice but to 'borrow' protein stores from elsewhere in the body to make up for the shortfall. Over time, particularly for people training for running events, this can mean a weakened immune system and can inhibit the body's ability to repair itself effectively. So, although you might not be in training for the world's strongest man/woman, try to ensure that you get good-quality protein into your diet. Good choices include:

- Lean cuts of meat, such as chicken, pork and beef (ideally steamed or stir fried, not roasted/fried)
- Fresh fish
- Eggs
- Dairy products (in moderation)
- Nuts and seeds
- Pulses and beans (which can easily be added to soups or salads)

Fat

The expanding waistlines of people in the western world can be blamed on a number of factors, ranging from lack of exercise to over-enthusiastic appetites. But if there was one food substance that was the main villain, fat would certainly be at the top of the list.

At 9 calories per gram, fat is the most calorific nutrient we can eat, making it largely responsible not only for our aesthetic imperfections, such as stubborn love handles and bingo wings, but also our inner health. Diets high in fat have long been known to play a major role in the onset of coronary heart disease, making it the one food substance we should make every effort to eat in moderation.

Although diets high in refined carbohydrate are also key players in causing a range of diseases, the abundance of fat in our diets really needs to be moderated if we are to enjoy the latter years of our life without suffering ill health.

The good news for you is that your training is having a major effect on keeping fat storage both on your hips and in your arteries at bay by using it as a source of energy, along with carbohydrates, to fuel your training runs. What's more, the fitter you get the more effective the body becomes at using fat as an energy source to fuel movement, so as time goes by your training is going to have a huge impact on

Expert corner

By eating a well-balanced diet, you should find that it contains sufficient quantities of protein to meet your daily requirements, but if you lead a hectic lifestyle and find yourself skipping the odd meal, it might be worth checking to see that you are getting enough.

Although the recommended requirements of protein vary from person to person, leading nutritionist Anita Bean suggests that endurance runners training moderately require around 1.2g of protein per kilogram of body weight. So, a 60kg runner should be looking to consume approximately 72g of protein a day.

To give you some idea of how much that is, here is the protein content of some popular foods:

- 130g chicken breast – 39g
- 100g tin of tuna – 24g
- 150g grilled mackerel – 31g
- 1 pint of skimmed milk – 20g
- 1 medium-sized egg – 10g
- 150g carton of plain yoghurt – 8g

those pesky areas on your body where you carry fat – be it your love handles, your thighs, your arms or your bum.

The good, the bad and the ugly

As evil as fat is for our arteries and waistlines, it does come in good forms, too, which we should eat on a regular basis.

The good: unsaturated fats

Unsaturated fats (such as those found in oily fish) contain what are commonly referred to as fatty acids, such as omega 3 and omega 6. These complex fatty acids are incredibly good for the body in a number of ways, such as helping to keep joints lubricated, improving brain function and helping the body fight inflammation. The more research that goes into unlocking the properties and secrets of essential fatty acids such as omega 3 and omega 6, the more health benefits scientists seem to uncover.

So, before you condemn all fatty foods to Room 101, try to make a conscious effort to eat foods rich in unsaturated fat, especially oily fish, at least twice a week, to help keep your heart and joints healthy. Good choices include:

• Salmon

• Mackerel

• Sardines

• Tuna steaks

• Flaxseed oil (ideal to drizzle over your salad)

• Rapeseed oil (also good with salad)

The bad: saturated fat

Unfortunately, it is the bad fats we should aim to avoid that are abundant in the western diet. Pizza, battered fish, curry, Chinese takeaway and pork sausages all contain their fair share of bad fat, and it doesn't take much to eat sufficient fat calories to give you enough energy to run a marathon.

Diets high in saturated fat have been scientifically proven to contribute to poor cardiovascular health, obesity, diabetes and high cholesterol, all of which are a ticket not only to reducing your life span but also to reducing your general quality of life.

The fact that you have chosen to train for and take part in a 5k or 10k run means that you have already found the perfect way to improve your cardiovascular health and lower your cholesterol levels. By reducing the amount of saturated fats you eat, you can help to double the positive effect that exercise has on your health, so why not use your 12 or so weeks of training as the ideal time to adopt a healthier way of living and cut out some (not all – you've got to have some vices) of the unnecessary saturated fats in your diet.

Sounds too difficult? It's easy when you know how. Why not try some of the following tips and you'll notice the difference in a matter of weeks.

• Trim off any unnecessary fat from pork/lamb chops.

• Substitute one or two fatty meals a week (such as bangers and mash or pizza) with healthy oily fish such as salmon or tuna with boiled new potatoes.

• Grill meat such as sausages, burgers, chops and steaks. You'll be amazed at how much fat you'll see drip off – it's better on the grill pan than in your arteries.

• Opt for lower-fat dairy produce such as skimmed milk. It might taste a bit bland initially, but after a few days your taste buds adjust and whole milk will taste like cream.

• Try to eat high-fat foods, such as butter, cream and cheese, sparingly – or choose lower-fat options.

- Replace a meat dish with a vegetarian meal once or twice a week to help boost your fibre intake and add variety to your diet.

All these tips are just tiny little adjustments you can make that you'll barely notice, yet over the course of a week you'll be reducing your calorie intake by thousands and, before you know it, combined with your training, any excess weight you are carrying will drop off.

The ugly: trans fats

If saturated fats are evil, then trans fats taught them all they know – because they are even worse. Trans fats are hidden in a range of foods from spreads to fast food, and are much harder to spot on labelling than saturated fats. Many products fail to make it

clear whether they contain trans fats, making it nearly impossible to know whether the biscuit or spread you are eating contains them.

If in doubt, the best thing to do is avoid any product that contains 'hydrogenated fat' as these will certainly contain trans fats.

Everything in moderation

Unless you are an elite athlete in training for an event where split seconds mean the difference between winning and losing, the need to obsess about everything that passes your lips is not completely necessary. As a first-time or novice runner with work commitments and/or a family to look after, you've got more than enough on your 'professional and social' plate than to overly concern yourself with whether you have met your daily requirements of protein, vegetables, carbohydrates and unsaturated fats.

The beauty of taking part in 5k and 10k events is that the distance you have to cover is nowhere near the physical limit that events such as the marathon push you to, where the importance of getting the right nutrition to fuel your run is vital.

For the majority of people reading this book, following a healthy and balanced diet, along with a few of the tips outlined in this chapter, is going to stand you in very good stead to train and race effectively, so try not to get yourself too bogged down in all the nutritional information that is available in book stores and on the internet. Nutrition as a whole, not just sports nutrition, is a minefield and you often find that the more you read and the more you learn, the more confusing and contradictory you will find the subject.

So, here are my top five tips on how you can improve the quality of your diet without having to become self sufficient or spending a small fortune:

- Vary the colour of the vegetables you eat to make sure you consume a variety of essential vitamins and minerals.

- Try to grill or steam meat or fish whenever possible. This will reduce its fat content and help you lose a little bit of unwanted weight – making running that much easier.

- Try to eat a different piece of fruit every day of the week rather than stick to your usual preference – apples and bananas for most people. Kiwi fruit, pears, melon, pineapple and strawberries are just a few examples of great tasting, yet often forgotten, fruits.

- When the option is available, swap white products with brown such as bread, rice and pasta. These wholegrain products have a higher fibre content and are a far better choice to keep your blood sugar levels stable.

- Experiment with different dishes, such as fish. Once you have successfully rustled up a healthy fish dish, you'll have the confidence to keep doing it and experiment further. Barbequed trout for example is as easy as steak, but many people are scared to give it a go.

A tip for smokers and drinkers

We all have our vices of one kind or another and although it's far from me to persuade you to give up the nation's two biggies – smoking and drinking – now that you're indulging in regular physical activity, it might be a good time to cut back on one (or both) of these vices.

Even though you may not suffer any direct ill effects in combining regular training with the occasional beer/wine and your usual 10–20 daily cigarettes, I can guarantee you'll find life so much easier on your waistline and lungs if you cut back even by just a little. The dehydrating effects of alcohol and the countless health hazards that smoking presents can make your training not only difficult, but in some cases potentially dangerous, so if you have wanted to find an excuse to quit or cut back on any of these vices, why not consider doing it now? There couldn't be a more appropriate time.

If you want to learn more about fuelling the body for running, I recommend *The Complete Guide to Sports Nutrition*, by Anita Bean (A&C Black). It covers everything you need to know and is an invaluable reference book for anyone interested in exploring the complex subject of sports nutrition.

⁝drink up

With so much going on in our hectic everyday lives, it's a sad fact that the vast majority of people simply forget to drink the one substance that is essential for keeping the body functioning. The number of clients I have had over the years who tell me that

The wonders of water

Despite containing no calories and relatively few nutrients, it's hard to believe how much of an effect water can have on the everyday functioning of our bodies at rest – let alone when exercising.

Now that you are subjecting yourself to regular, sweat-inducing exercise three times a week, here are a few water facts that you might find interesting – and that will, I hope, incentivise you to take your fluids seriously.

they either haven't had time to drink water or that they just 'forgot' to drink is staggering, especially when you consider that water is arguably the most important substance our bodies need to survive.

- The human body consists of around 60–70 per cent water.

- During a 10k race in warm conditions you could easily lose 1 litre of fluid through sweat and respiration.

- Of our total daily intake of fluid, 60 per cent comes from water, 30 per cent from food and 10 per cent from the metabolic reactions within our body.

- During a long run such as a marathon, it is not uncommon to lose 6–8 per cent of body water content despite taking on fluids during the race.

- A 2 per cent drop in hydration status leads to a significant rise in heart rate and core body temperature.

- A 5 per cent drop in hydration status can lead to a 30 per cent reduction in prolonged aerobic capacity.

- The muscles of a runner's legs can produce as much as 250ml of fluid in as little as 1–2 hours.

Getting the drinks in

In training or not, knowing exactly how much you should be drinking every day is not always easy, but it's something you really should find out. Keeping the body hydrated is essential for many reasons – for example, to help the kidneys perform their job of filtering out metabolic waste products effectively and, for runners, to keep the muscles well lubricated and contracting smoothly.

With huge variations in each individual's metabolic requirements, activity levels and how hot or humid the day is, it is nearly impossible to give a generic figure and say with any certainty that they should be drinking 'x' number of litres of water every day. The

What to drink?

Courtesy of the press, we are frequently bombarded with contradictory advice on what qualifies as a 'hydrating' fluid. One week we are told that water is the only drink we should consider, but the very next week we are told that, actually, coffee and tea are just as effective at hydrating us. So which advice should you follow?

Ideally, you should get the vast majority of your daily fluid from water rather than rely on PG Tips and Nescafé to hydrate you. However, provided you pass the pee test, it shows that you are well hydrated and I wouldn't lose too much sleep over it.

good news, however, is that there is an easy way to tell if you are sufficiently hydrated, simply by visiting the bathroom ...

The pee test

This is an easy test to carry out, and incredibly useful in terms of giving you a good indicator of how hydrated you are.

The next time you visit the bathroom, all you need to do is take a look at the colour of your urine. If it is dark yellow in colour, this indicates that you are dehydrated. If it is running clear or a pale straw-like colour, it indicates that you are sufficiently hydrated.

Although you are likely to always be dehydrated first thing in the morning, you should try to make sure that, throughout the day, you drink sufficient quantities of fluid (be it water, tea, juice or milk) to keep your urine running a pale colour. Staying hydrated throughout the day will not only keep your kidneys happy but will also ensure that your muscles are ready and willing to take on a training run.

Timing your fluid intake

Keeping yourself hydrated is one thing, but the challenge of getting the timing of your fluid intake right over your months of training can be quite tricky. Drink too much just before a training run and your stomach will feel like a washing machine; drink too little hours before a run and you can find yourself parched and gasping for water after just 10 minutes.

The best advice is to simply try to keep yourself hydrated throughout the day, rather than guzzle down a litre of water an hour before a training run. Keeping your body constantly well hydrated will ensure you are ready to run whenever you fancy it, keep your concentration up throughout the day and make it that much easier for your kidneys to do their job.

As a rough guide, use the following pointers to give you an idea of the quantities and timings of fluid intake before and during training:

- 400–600ml (¾ to 1 pint) 2 hours before a run
- 150–300ml (¼ to ½ a pint) in the last 20 minutes before a run (or 6 ml per kg of body weight)
- 150–250ml (¼ to just under ½ a pint) every 15–20 minutes during the run, particularly on warm days

A tip for early risers

For all you early-bird runners who like to get your training sessions over and done with first thing in the morning, hydrating yourself before you hit the pavement can be a bit tricky.

As you'll see from the colour of your urine, you are dehydrated in the morning and if you are about to embark on physical exercise, even if it's just a 20-minute power walk, getting some fluids on board is essential. The best advice is to take small but regular sips of water as soon as you wake up. Try to rise early enough so that you can allow at least 20–30 minutes before you start running, making sure any fluid you take on is consumed in small sips rather than big glugs. Big mouthfuls can trap air and make your stomach feel very uncomfortable.

If you find it difficult to hydrate yourself well enough in the morning, you could always consider taking a special running water bottle with you on your training run. Although some runners find them a little cumbersome and difficult to jog with, they are an ideal solution to addressing the hydration problem for morning joggers.

Sports drinks: worth it or worthless?

Brightly coloured, sweet-tasting sports drinks are big business, and runners in particular have developed a great fondness of them over the years.

What's in a sports drink?

A typical 500 millilitre sports drink (just under a pint) will contain approximately:

- 140 calories
- 32 grams of carbohydrate
- 0 grams of fat

All brands of sports drink, from Lucozade to Boost, claim their drinks can help you run faster for longer – but are they actually that much more effective than water at hydrating the body and giving you the extra energy boost they promise to deliver?

How they work

The science behind how sports drinks benefit the body is actually quite simple and will help you make up your own mind as to whether, you should be drinking them over the course of your training.

Although sports drinks come in a number of forms, by far the most popular, and the type you will see on the supermarket shelves, are 'isotonic' sports drinks. All this means is that they contain very similar amounts of sugar and salts as our own body fluids, making them a little more effective at being absorbed faster in the gut than normal water.

Faster hydration means that essential 'performance sustaining' fluid reaches your cells and muscles in the quickest possible time, helping you to keep going during your training sessions.

Sounds great doesn't it? Why bother with water when you can get so much more from a sweet-tasting sports drink?

The truth is that, although isotonic sports drinks have been proven to help improve the speed at which the body is hydrated and to help improve endurance, these benefits are not really applicable to runners training for 5k and 10k events.

Leading sports nutritionist Anita Bean makes it clear that sports drinks certainly benefit people undertaking moderate or high-intensity sporting events lasting longer than an hour, and research certainly backs this up. However, for events lasting less than an hour, or those performed at a low intensity (around 60–70 per cent of HR max), isotonic sports drinks have no significant performance-enhancing benefits. Marathon runners will certainly see the benefits of choosing isotonic sports drinks over water during their long training runs but, unless you are training in very hot weather for long periods of time, water will be just as effective.

The choice is yours

Despite the fact that the science may not be in the favour of isotonic sports drinks for 5k and 10k runners, this doesn't necessarily mean that they will do you any harm if you choose to drink them over water. Although research at Birmingham University discovered that they contribute to dissolving tooth enamel, and this is a warning sign that they should be consumed only in moderation, there is certainly no harm in indulging in a sports drink every now and again, particularly on warm days.

If the temptation is too great and you choose to use isotonic sports drinks regularly before, during and after a run, here is a word of caution if you were hoping that your training was going to melt away those love handles: at around 150 calories a bottle, you're going to have to cover well over a mile before you burn off those calories – so a bottle before and after training is nearly 5k worth of calories.

❖nutritional supplements – friend or foe?

Much to the dismay of the bulk of the orthodox medical community and the delight of the proponents of alternative and natural therapies, the UK has become a nation of nutritional supplement pill poppers.

For the past couple of decades we have developed a fascination and trust in what nutritional supplements such as vitamins, minerals, algaes and herbs have to offer our immune systems, energy levels and even libidos, causing the industry to be worth billions and our kitchen cabinets to be full of brightly coloured bottles.

Of course, the claimed immune-boosting and health improving properties of nutritional supplements are not shared by everyone, with large sections of the medical community being very outspoken in their opinion that they are nothing more than a waste of money. These proclamations however have not made a jot of difference to our love affair with natural supplements and there certainly doesn't seem to be any sign of us falling out of love anytime soon.

Whichever side of the argument you find yourself, you'd probably be lying if you said you'd never bought yourself the odd bottle of vitamin C or fish oil capsules. We've all dabbled at some stage of our lives (usually when our heads and chests are full of cold in the winter), but now that you are training for a 5k or 10k race you might be wondering if any specific supplements may help you get the most out of your body during your long weeks of training.

There is certainly no shortage of supplements to choose from, with many specifically marketed for active people, but will they actually do you any good or possibly even do you harm?

The subject of vitamin and mineral supplementation is complex but there are one or two things you need to know before you start gobbling down your zinc and calcium supplements like smarties.

Synergy – vitamins and minerals working together

The principle of synergy is perhaps the most important concept you need to understand when it comes to vitamin supplementation. Although it is easy (far too easy according to some medical professionals) to walk into a health food store and fill your boots with whatever vitamin or mineral takes your fancy or supplement you read about in the Sunday papers, it is essential that you understand that they do not work well on their own.

All vitamins have what are known as synergists, which they must work with to fulfil a certain bodily function. Synergists, put simply, are other vitamins and minerals which team up with others to carry out certain physiological functions to maximum effect. No single vitamin can work individually and carry out its job unless it is helped by one or more of its, shall we say, 'partners in crime'.

Perfect examples of this include:

- Iron is not nearly as effectively absorbed into the blood stream without the help of vitamin C and zinc.
- In order for vitamin B6 to be effective you need to have sufficient zinc levels. If you are deficient in zinc, B6 is not anywhere near as effective at performing its biological role as it should be.

- We need adequate levels of vitamin D in the body to aid in the absorption of calcium: without vitamin D, calcium is next to useless.

Know the risks

The overview of the vitamins that follows is included as a guide and not a list of supplements I suggest you head out and buy after reading this chapter. The subject of nutritional supplementation is far more complex than most people realise and despite their ease of availability, even the most innocent and common of vitamins have the ability to adversely interact with prescribed pharmaceutical medication you may be taking or with certain existing medical conditions you may have.

Therefore, even though any health food store owner will happily sell you a bottle of innocent looking magnesium or calcium tablets in exchange for a five pound note, it does not mean it is wise for you to take them, and a consultation with your GP is strongly advised.

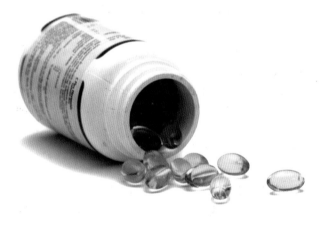

Dangerous interactions

The list of the potentially dangerous interactions between nutritional supplements and more conventional medication is extensive, but here are a few common interactions which might make you think twice about popping pills willy-nilly.

Vitamin E and warfarin

Warfarin is a common drug prescribed by GPs to help thin the blood and assists in preventing blood clotting and therefore thrombosis. However, the supplement vitamin E can be purchased in every health food store can also thin the blood, potentially leading to excessively thin blood, very easy bruising and potentially serious health complications.

Vitamin B12 and potassium

Even if you are not taking any other forms of medication and thought you were safe from any dangerous health implications from taking supplements, think again. If you take potassium supplements for long enough, it can have a depleting effect on your B12 levels and lead to a condition known as pernicious anaemia.

Thyroxine and kelp

If you have been diagnosed with an underactive thyroid gland and have been prescribed thyroxine, it is essential that you speak with your GP if you are considering taking a number of natural food supplements, such as sea kelp or iodine. These also have an effect on the thyroid gland and can cause ill health if taken together.

The low down on the top running supplements

There are dozens of supplements you could be convinced to buy to help you get the most out of your body for your upcoming training, but the following six are the ones I believe you may have considered, or will be advised to consider, purchasing.

Once again, this is not a shopping list of supplements I recommend you buy, it is simply an overview of some common supplements which will help give you a little more information about what they do and how they could help – or hinder – your training.

The following are the most popular supplements runners purchase:

- Vitamin C
- B vitamins
- Zinc
- Omega-3 fish oils
- Magnesium
- Calcium

Vitamin C

Vitamin C is perhaps the most widely taken of nutritional supplements and comes in many different forms from 'timed release' preparations to ones with added 'bioflavanoids'.

The varieties available can get really confusing, especially when the amount of vitamin C each capsule provides can range from as little as 60mg to a massive 1500mg.

What it does

Whatever preparation you choose, the ultimate benefits of vitamin C are to help boost your immune system, reform collagen (essential after an injury, as it helps the body to manufacture new tissue to repair damaged ligaments and tendons) and to serve as a potent anti-oxidant – which is particularly important if you are exercising regularly.

Possible side effects

Provided you do not exceed the recommended dose indicated on the bottle you should not experience any side effects. However, some people are sensitive to the ascorbic acid that makes up the vitamin C capsule, giving them symptoms of diarrhoea.

Vitamin C food sources

Fruit (particularly citrus), vegetables and potatoes.

Conclusion

Vitamin C is an incredibly common supplement and can generally be used safely for people of all ages. In fact, it has been proven to have the added benefits of

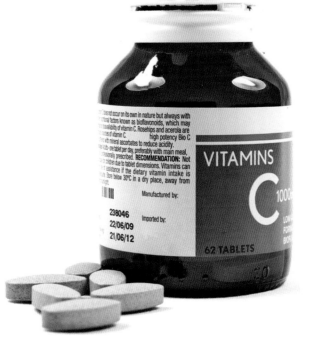

aiding the absorption of iron into the blood stream, making it the perfect partner for those with low iron levels or people who have been advised to take supplementary iron preparations.

B Vitamins

Due to the number of B vitamins, it's easier to give you an overview of them as a group, rather than individually. The family of B vitamins are also known as 'B complex' and include a large number of nutrients. Although there is some debate about which ones fit into the family, the main ones include:

- B1 – Thiamine
- B2 – Riboflavin
- B3 – Niacin
- B5 – Pantothenic acid
- B6 – Pyridoxine
- B12 – Cobalamin
- Biotin
- Folic acid

There are also vitamins B15 and B17, but they are not widely available in supplement form.

What they do

B vitamins have a key part in energy production. Put simply, if you are low in B vitamins you won't have the energy to train. Provided you eat a well-balanced diet rich in whole grains it is unlikely you will be deficient, but that doesn't stop thousands of people every year buying a bottle or two of B complex in hope of the advertised 'energy boost'. Certain individual B vitamins are also essential in making us feel generally healthier. For example, vitamin B6 has a vital role in the manufacture of red blood cells and new proteins. His partners in crime are vitamins B12 and folic acid, as they also have a part to play in the production of red blood cells in the bone marrow.

Possible side effects

As with all vitamin and mineral supplements, provided you have spoken to your GP about any possible interaction supplements may have with medication you are taking or existing medical conditions such as kidney or heart problems, B vitamins are safe to take if you follow the dosage guidelines.

Taking excessive quantities of B complex or individual B vitamins can result in a number of side effects which include turning your urine bright yellow, a 'blushing' of the cheeks if you take too much B3, and restlessness at night in cases of excessive quantities of B6.

B vitamin food sources

Vegetables, salads, whole grains, meats, eggs.

Conclusion

B-complex vitamins are very popular supplements and are, generally speaking, safe supplements to take as they are water soluble. Being water soluble, any excess that you consume is passed through the body (via your urine) within a few hours so they pose little risk of building up and becoming toxic. However, they still have the potential to cause nasty side effects if you exceed the stated dose.

Now that you're training for a 5k or 10k race and you're more active now than you have probably been in years, there may be an increased need for B complex, but before you do go down the pill-popping route, make sure your diet is of high quality first. In most cases, it's far cheaper, safer and more effective to obtain your vitamins from the food you eat than rely on pills.

The intriguing thing people notice about B vitamins is their individual availability in health food stores. They are available either as 'B complex' or as individual supplements such as B6 or B12, which

usually come in higher doses. Although there are some cases where taking extra supplemental B vitamins, such as B6 for symptoms of PMS, can be beneficial, if in doubt, it's always best to take B complex. This way you can get maximum benefit from all the B's and their synergists. Like most vitamins, the Bs are most effective when they are consumed with their synergists, so it is therefore strongly advised that before you load up your basket with individual B vitamins (or vitamins of any kind) you first of all speak to someone who knows which vitamins are best for you and if they are actually necessary.

Zinc

Zinc is commonly taken together with vitamin C in the winter time to help give the immune system a boost and according to many top nutritionists, such as Patrick Holford, founder of the Institute of Optimum Nutrition, maybe it's a good thing too. It is thought that a large percentage of us simply don't get enough zinc from our daily diet, making us all deficient in one degree or another. With your exercise levels now at an all-year high, your immune system may very well need a boost and zinc could help if you felt you needed it.

What it does

Zinc plays a number of key roles in the body, including the complex manufacture of essential enzymes and the protection and repair of our DNA. These roles help to keep our immune system strong and assist in the regulation of important hormones known as prostaglandins.

Without adequate levels of zinc, we cannot live our everyday lives with the zing we'd like, let alone run three times a week, so it's really important you eat a well-balanced diet rich in meat, seafood, wheatgerm and eggs.

Possible side effects

There are generally no major side effects if you take too much zinc, but you run the risk of disrupting the balance of other vitamins and minerals such as iron and copper if you exceed the recommended dose.

Zinc food sources

Seafood, oysters, eggs, meat, pumpkin seeds.

Expert corner

A good way to see if you might be deficient in zinc is to take a look at your nails.

According to world-renowned nutritionist Patrick Holford, if you notice that one or two of your finger nails have white marks on them and you think your sense of taste and smell is not what it should be, there is a strong chance that you have a deficiency in zinc.

Conclusion

Zinc is a really important mineral for everyone and with many experts believing most of us are deficient in it, it's crucial we ensure that our diets are packed full of it. With so many vital roles in the body, from regulating the manufacture of enzymes and hormones to its essential synergistic role with other nutrients, zinc is a nutrient you really shouldn't be deficient in. When you consider that up to 3mg can be lost per day through your sweat, runners should be particularly vigilant about ensuring they are getting enough.

Omega 3 and fish oil

Going into the extremely complex world of unsaturated fats and essential fatty acids is way beyond the scope of this book, but a few facts about the benefits of omega-3 fatty acids are certainly

worth mentioning. This subject of the omegas (3, 6 and 9) and their role in the body is fascinating and every year scientists find out about them. Omega 3 however, is perhaps the most read about essential fatty acid (EFA) and one which is readily available as fish oil in all health food stores.

What it does

Omega 3 comes in a variety of forms, but ultimately the body uses it for a range of functions including:

- regulation of hormones
- reduce inflammation
- manufacture essential prostaglandins
- aid the immune system.

In addition and of particular importance to anyone who exercises regularly omega 3 also has the following effect on the body:

- improved aerobic metabolism
- improved stamina and energy levels
- improved ability for the body to deliver oxygen to the working muscle cells.

Possible side effects

It is unlikely that you'll overdose on omega 3 if you follow the guidelines.

Omega-3 food sources

Any oily fish such as salmon, mackerel, sardines and tuna.

To maximise your omega-3 intake, make sure the fish is fresh and not canned, as the process can extract out the beneficial omega-3 oils.

Conclusion

Although it is impossible to put a figure on, in my experience there are a lot of people who take supplementary omega-3 without really understanding the exact reasons why they are taking it. Omega-3 supplements are very expensive and often unnecessary if you eat a diet rich in oily fish. There is no doubt that the vast majority of people could do with more omega 3 in their diets, but supplementation is not always the answer.

Magnesium

Magnesium is classed as a 'macro mineral' and is therefore an essential mineral that we should avoid being deficient in at all costs. The fact that it is a major component of our bones and teeth should give you an idea of just how important it is.

What it does

Magnesium works in conjunction with calcium to not only keep our bones strong but to also oversee proper nerve and muscle function. Without adequate levels of magnesium, our muscles would be susceptible to weakness and painful muscle spasms and our cardiovascular systems would not be nearly as efficient as they should be – two essential functions you need for performing well if you're training for a 5k or 10k race!

Possible side effects

Magnesium is abundant in a healthy and well-balanced diet so there should not be any reason to supplement with extra magnesium tablets, thereby running the risk of taking too much. However, the main danger you are exposed to if you take excessive quantities of magnesium for long periods of time is causing an imbalance with calcium. Caution should also be exercised for those with kidney problems or those taking diuretic medication.

Magnesium food sources

Green leafy vegetables, nuts and seeds, figs.

Conclusion

Magnesium, like all other macro minerals, is essential for normal bodily functions but its influence on the functioning of our skeletal and cardiac muscles and nerves clearly demonstrates how important it is for people who run. Although our bodies are able to efficiently store over 20 grams of magnesium and call upon it to enter the blood stream whenever it is needed, it is still vital that we consume sufficient amounts so that our muscles and nerves can function optimally.

Calcium

Like magnesium, calcium is known as a macro nutrient. It works in conjunction with magnesium and performs similar roles in the body, particularly in the maintenance of proper muscle and nerve function.

What it does

We all know that calcium is a vital component of bone but it also plays a major part in ensuring that our skeletal and cardiac muscles contract properly to ensure our heart keeps beating and our legs keep moving.

As a runner, calcium is really important because if you are deficient it can have serious consequences on your bone density. For women, it is especially important that your diet is rich in calcium as you are more likely to be deficient in it that men.

Possible side effects

Although the importance of consuming adequate levels of calcium cannot be underestimated, it is just as important to ensure you don't buy calcium supplements and eat them as though they are smarties. Taking large doses of calcium can cause an imbalance with magnesium and phosphorus so it is recommended that you avoid calcium supplementation if you are lead to believe that you may be deficient in either.

Calcium food sources

Dairy produce, sardines, salmon, green vegetables, nuts and seeds.

Conclusion

As you can see, it is nearly impossible to know if you are doing the right thing for your body by supplementing it with extra calcium – or any food supplement. With so many variables and possible interactions caused by popping an innocent-looking pill you'll always be wondering if you have done the right thing.

Generally speaking, although it might sound like a broken record, for those people who eat a balanced diet rich in fish, vegetables and dairy you should be getting adequate amounts of calcium without the need for supplementation.

Expert corner

Unfortunately, simply eating or supplementing your diet with minerals such as magnesium or calcium doesn't necessarily guarantee that your body will be able to efficiently absorb them. Calcium is the perfect example. Substances known as 'oxalates' and 'phytates', which can be found in vegetable and grain products respectively, actually inhibit absorption of the mineral into the intestine. So, if you think your body is getting all its daily calcium allowance from the milk splashed over your wholegrain cereal in the morning, think again.

Coffee, cocoa, alcohol and fatty foods are also guilty of inhibiting mineral absorption so it's a good idea to obtain your daily requirement of nutrients from a number of sources, rather than relying on just one.

Giving in to temptation

Despite all the information I have just given you on the potential side effects and questionable necessity of supplementing your training with food supplements, many of you will give in to temptation and stock that kitchen cabinet with a decent spread of vitamin and mineral pills and potions to give you an extra edge during your hard weeks of training. This decision is of course yours and one which I neither condemn or endorse; all I suggest is that you be aware of all the potential side effects that food supplements can have and be extra cautious if you are taking any medication prescribed by your GP.

Taken in the correct quantities for the appropriate deficiencies or ailments, I'll be the first to admit that vitamin and mineral supplements have their benefits and can give some people huge improvements in health. Iron supplements for people who are anaemic and zinc for people with weak immune systems can make huge strides in improving well-being, but taken incorrectly and they can easily cause more problems than they cure.

If you are genuinely of the belief that you could benefit from taking supplements, I suggest you make an appointment with a qualified nutritionist who will be able to advise you on what supplements you need and which ones you should avoid. It's an information minefield out there and although good old Google or Yahoo can give you an idea of what nutritional deficiencies you may have, the quality of information can be patchy and sometimes grossly inaccurate.

I sincerely hope you are able to get the most out of your body for your upcoming 5k or 10k race and that for every training run you do you are bursting with energy and eagerly looking forward to your next session. Although a positive mindset and a good eight hours of sleep every night are two key ingredients you need for this spring in your step, the importance of your diet cannot be ignored.

Good quality nutrition is vital if you are to have the energy to live your everyday life and train – but relying on pills in a selection of bottles in your kitchen is not the answer. Nutritional supplements are there to 'supplement' your diet, not replace it.

Further reading on food supplements

For more information on the fascinating world of nutrition and food supplements the following books are well worth reading.

- *The Complete Guide to Sports Nutrition and Sports Supplements: Which Nutritional Supplements Really Work* by Anita Bean (A&C Black)
- *The Optimum Nutrition Bible* by Patrick Holford (Piatkus)
- *The Vitamin Bible* by Earl Mindell (Arlington Books)

10 running repairs

New jogger or running veteran – it doesn't matter what level of experience you have, picking up injuries is, sadly, one of the occupational hazards you have to get used to as part of your race preparations. Some runners are lucky and seem to have a built-in immunity to any kind of muscle twinge or niggle, but most of us can pick up an injury at any stage of training, and it can be incredibly frustrating.

prevention is better than cure

If you haven't already, I strongly suggest you read through Chapter 7 now, to see how easy it is to avoid picking up common injuries in the first place. By performing some basic exercises, which you can do while watching TV, you can keep certain muscles strong and this in turn will help to keep your body well balanced during the running stride. Of course, these exercises do not prevent you from picking up all injuries but they are a good place to start.

Along with the exercises, there are a number of other steps you can take to try to avoid those annoying injuries that can end up bugging you for the duration of your training. Some of these measures have been explained in the book already, but in case you glossed over them, here are my top five injury-prevention tips.

1. Get your running gait analysed

Often overlooked by 5k and 10k runners as something that only marathon runners should worry about, getting your running gait analysed is essential to keeping you injury free. Through gait analysis, you can make sure that the trainers you buy to run in are both comfortable and perfectly matched to your running style.

2. Take one step at a time

Being enthusiastic about your training is fantastic, but try not to get ahead of yourself. Upping your running distance too soon, or running too fast when your body isn't conditioned for it, is a recipe for injury, so try to keep your enthusiasm in check by increasing training intensity gradually.

3. Stretch regularly

As boring as it might be to spend 20 minutes each day stretching out your leg muscles, it is vital if you want to prevent picking up niggles. By keeping your muscles well stretched you can make sure that your muscle fibres are always ready to take on a training run, and at the same time reduce any tension on your joints.

4. Vary your training

They say variety is the spice of life, but it's also a great way to reduce your injury risk. Although the majority of your training will involve power walking, jogging or running, it's a good idea to change disciplines every now and again and head out for a swim or bike ride. The change will be welcomed by your leg muscles, as they are given a respite from the repetitive nature of running, while, at the same time, the change of activity will keep your interest up.

5. If in doubt: rest

Depending on your race aspirations, for some of you the advice to embrace rest will be welcome. Although you should not, of course, get too carried away with rest days, it is equally important that you shouldn't feel the need to train every day. Some runners get too carried away with training and can end up doing too much, leading to overuse injuries and forced time off running.

At times, rest is good – especially if you feel a muscle niggle coming on. Nip it in the bud early and you save yourself weeks of injury-related frustration.

·:·avoiding 'environmental injuries'

Say the word 'injury' and it automatically conjures up an image of someone limping and holding an ice pack on their leg, but not all running injuries are caused by pulled muscles or knee pain picked up halfway through a run.

Whether you anticipate running on roads, along forest trails or in the local park there are dozens of environmental hazards around every corner, so it's important to bear in the mind the following things the next time you head out for a run.

Here comes the sun

Slapping on sunscreen before a run is often the last thing on your mind, but strong sun can pack a punch on your pasty winter-white nose and shoulders. Even if you are only heading out for a short run, if the sun is shining and your skin is exposed it is essential you take just a few minutes to slap on some high factor sunscreen to protect your skin from sunburn. For more information on the dangers of over exposure to the sun and how to protect yourself in the sun visit Cancer Research UK's SunSmart campaign website at www.sunsmart.org.uk.

Rickety roads

When you've got over the difficult early weeks of your running training, where you feel constantly out of breath, your confidence grows and you find that

your training sessions get far more enjoyable. The trouble is, often with extra confidence comes complacency, and as enjoyable as it is taking in the spring daffodils on your daily jog, pot holes, uneven ground and hidden tree roots can all spring a nasty surprise upon you.

All it takes is one of these innocuous features to suddenly appear underfoot and, through no fault of your own, you can end up with a twisted ankle or an up-close-and-personal meeting with the pavement. Although bad luck is often to blame for these kinds of injuries, it's still a good idea to make mental notes of hazardous areas on your running route and be extra vigilant on new routes.

Feeling hot, hot, hot

As you are training for a 5k or 10k, you'll notice from your training plans that the furthest you really need to run in training is 10k – or just over in some cases.

On this basis, you should never find yourself far from home, but when it's a hot day and something goes wrong, be it fatigue, the heat or an injury, 5k away from home can seem like miles. Although it's

not advisable to run in the middle of the day when the thermometer is reading well into 80°F (25°C) it's a good idea to take precautions if you find yourself in a pickle. A mobile, a fiver, a few coins and a water bottle are just a few small things you can take with you that don't weigh much but could come in very handy if you run into trouble.

Lastly, as obvious as it might sound, wear as little as possible on hot days to avoid overheating. Over the years I have noticed that far too many runners insist on wearing long trousers and long-sleeved tops on hot days, when shorts and a vest would be more appropriate. Overheating can be serious for runners, so try to stay as cool as possible.

❖ diagnosing and treating common injuries

You can take all the precautions you like, from religiously doing the exercises outlined in Chapter 7 to taking more than your fair share of rest days, but sometimes, no matter what you do, you fall victim to an injury.

Veteran runners who have thousands of miles under their belts often see injuries as a sort of 'badge of honour', but newcomers to the world of running see them as nothing more than a pain in the derriere – sometimes quite literally.

Running injuries come in a variety of forms, some of which are acute (short term) some chronic (long term), but as frustrating as they are, always remember that they are all curable and, with good management, the majority of injuries will heal quickly and you'll be back on the road before you know it.

Seek professional advice

This section of the book will help you to diagnose and, to a degree, treat some of the most common injuries that afflict runners – but do not rely on it as your sole method of diagnosis and treatment. Going into great depth about injuries is beyond the scope of this book, so my advice is to always seek professional advice from a physiotherapist or sports therapist if an injury persists for more than a few days. If you leave injuries untreated for too long, this simply delays the healing process, and an untreated niggle that is 'bread and butter' to an injury specialist can end up taking weeks to heal, severely affecting your training regime and sometimes ending your hopes of competing in the race.

No matter what your hopes are for your 5k or 10k – be it walking, jogging or running the course, they are all far more fun than hobbling around it. So do yourself a favour and get your injury assessed and treated by an expert – it's worth the investment.

Expert corner

In a world where there is a pill for nearly every ill, pain relief from most injuries is often no further away than a few ibuprofen tablets. However, relying on non-steroidal anti-inflammatory drugs (NSAIDs) too regularly or for too long may affect your long-term health, so try to use them sparingly. Excessive and chronic use of NSAIDs can lead to stomach bleeding and stomach ulcers.

Leading joint pain specialist Dr Gordon Cameron claims that 25 million stronger NSAID prescriptions are issued in the UK each year, resulting in 2000 admissions to hospital to treat serious side effects, and as many as 2600 overdoses.

The top five most common running injuries

You don't have to search very hard to find dozens of books on how to prevent, diagnose and treat injuries, so if you are one of those unfortunate runners that is injury prone, and you find yourself picking up a few too many aches and pains, I strongly suggest you both invest in an in-depth book on injuries and seek professional advice.

I hope that, with the help of all the advice you have read in this book, you will avoid picking up any injuries but, if you do fall victim to one, it is likely that you will be afflicted by one of the following top five common running injuries:

- Pulled muscles
- Achilles tendonitis

- Shin splints
- ITB syndrome
- Blisters

We will now take a look at each of these.

Pulled muscles

Pulled muscles, most of the time, are very avoidable injuries, particularly for runners, provided that you stretch well and don't make any sudden movements that put cold muscles under stress.

Causes

Pulled muscles in runners usually affect one of three muscles: the groin, the hamstring or the calf. Although they can occur at any time, if you are going to pull a muscle it will either happen at the start of

the run, when your muscles are still relatively cold, when running up a hill – when the muscles are all of a sudden put under a little more strain – or at the end of a run, when you kick for home and ask your already tired muscles for a little bit more oomph.

Symptoms

In explosive sports such as football, rugby and sprinting, a pulled muscle will feel like a 'ping', followed by a lot of pain as large numbers of fibres tear, but for 5k and 10k runners it is more likely that you'll feel a sudden sharp pain in the affected muscle, making running very uncomfortable. In milder cases, it might just feel a little sore in the muscle but not so severe that you feel you have to stop running. Either way, these symptoms indicate that you have strained a muscle, so you should stop running and get it treated.

Treatment

As soon as you think you have a pulled muscle the very first thing you must do is adopt the RICE protocol:

R Rest the injury
I Ice the area with a bag of cold peas (do not place directly on to the skin, though – wrap it in a tea towel first)
C Compress the muscle with a bandage
E Elevate the injury to reduce blood flow to the area

In most cases, following these simple steps for a few days will see the muscle strain heal up nicely, and certainly within a week it will be repaired well enough to head out for a light jog.

Always make sure you stretch regularly after a muscle pull, but be careful not to be too aggressive with the stretch. Gently does it.

Achilles tendonitis

The Achilles tendon is the long, thick tendon which connects the heel bone to the calf muscle. This is a particularly nasty injury and one you really want to avoid picking up. It is an incredibly stubborn injury and, once you've got it, it can take weeks to shake it off.

Causes

Fortunately, Achilles tendonitis is very avoidable. Provided you follow all of the advice in this book in terms of choosing the right trainers for your gait and increasing the intensity of your training gradually. Achilles tendonitis usually affects runners who not only wear the wrong footwear but also get too ambitious with their training schedule, and either increase their mileage too fast or overdo hard training sessions, thereby placing excessive strain on an already hard-working muscle/tendon that simply isn't ready for it.

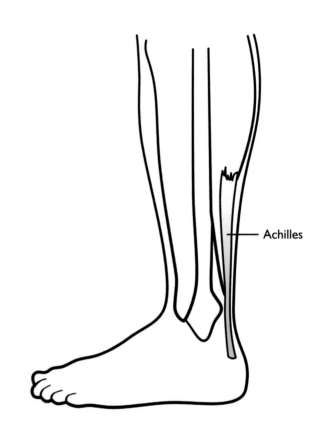

Achilles

Symptoms

- Stiffness in the Achilles tendon, especially in the morning
- Pain when trying to stand on tip-toe and/or walking upstairs
- Gradual onset of discomfort during and after exercise
- Significant tenderness when touching the Achilles
- Swelling in the tendon

Treatment

The frustrating thing about an Achilles injury over most others is the difficulty you have in trying to rest it. The Achilles tendon is used every time you walk, so it's very difficult to stop using it to give it a chance to heal. The best way to treat it is to:

- follow the RICE protocol – Rest, Ice, Compression, Elevation;
- avoid actions or situations that elicit pain;
- only perform exercise that does not aggravate it – swimming is a good option, using mainly the upper body.

It's best to act fast at the first sign of an Achilles injury by icing it regularly. If you nip it in the bud early on, you can avoid long-term problems with a sore Achilles, so the old adage 'a stitch in time saves nine' could not be more apt than in this case.

The dreaded stitch

No matter how fit you are, at some stage during your training it is likely that you will be afflicted by the dreaded runners' stitch.

A stitch is a sharp pain, usually felt on the right side of your abdomen, and can travel all the way up to your shoulder. The pain can be so great that it often forces runners to stop running, and sometimes lying down on the floor is the only way to alleviate the symptoms. Once you have a stitch it can be very difficult to get rid of while out running, so the best advice I can give aims to help you avoid getting one in the first place. The exact cause of a stitch is still largely unknown, but scientists have come up with a few pointers on how to reduce your chances of getting one.

- Try not to eat or drink large volumes of food 2–3 hours before a run.
- Try to have a bowel movement before heading out for a training session.
- Avoid long periods of running downhill, as this can spark off a stitch.
- Try to 'belly breathe' – that is, draw in air all the way to the stomach, rather than just to your lungs.
- Keep your stomach muscles strong by performing core stomach exercises.

Shin splints

Shin splints are very common, especially with those who are new to running. Put simply, any discomfort (usually muscular) you feel in the lower leg – either at the side, middle or the front – is likely to be a form of shin splint. Often it can be so painful that even walking, let alone jogging, is not a comfortable experience, so a period of rest from training is often the only answer.

Causes

In most cases, runners pick up shin splints when their lower leg muscles are working at an intensity that they are simply not used to, causing minor inflammation and tenderness in the soft tissue around the shin area. This is often the reason why new runners suffer the most, so if you are just starting out make sure you take your time with your training and up your running distance gradually.

Other common causes include:

- a sudden change in running surface;
- a sudden increase in running speed;
- the introduction of hill training, putting stress on the lower leg muscles;
- running in the wrong shoes for your running gait.

Symptoms

Most symptoms of shin splints show themselves a day or two after running, where you'll experience discomfort in your lower leg. Often, just touching the

muscle next to the shin bone is painful, but rest assured that the pain often dissipates after a few days.

Other signs include:

- pain when you draw your feet upwards;
- pain when walking up a hill.

Treatment

Most of the time, good old rest is the best medicine for shin splints. Provided you have done everything you can in terms of wearing the right trainers and not pushing yourself too hard on your training runs, most of the time shin splints are acute and will heal up in a matter of days.

In some cases, special shoe inserts called 'orthotics' are needed to correct any lower-leg biomechanical problems you might have. Orthotics are specially made inserts which you place in your running shoes to help correct over-pronation (your foot rolling inwards). Many runners swear by orthotics and claim they have helped them to overcome a range of injuries from shin splints to Achilles tendonitis, but these can be very expensive and they are often unnecessary.

Illio-tibial band (ITB) syndrome

In joint first place with Achilles tendonitis as the most stubborn of running injuries, illio-tibial band, or ITB, syndrome is another injury you really must avoid picking up. It is a very difficult one to treat and often ruins any hopes that runners have of competing in their chosen event.

This condition occurs as a result of a long fibrous band of tissue on the outside of your leg becoming excessively tight, causing inflammation and pain, often on the outside of the knee but it can also affect the area around the outer side of your hip.

Causes

There are a number of causes of ITB syndrome and it can affect any runner regardless of their sex, age or fitness levels. The main causes include:

- running on a cambered or uneven surface;
- upping your running mileage too quickly;
- increasing the intensity of your runs;
- wearing incorrect running shoes for your gait;
- muscular imbalance in the leg muscles.

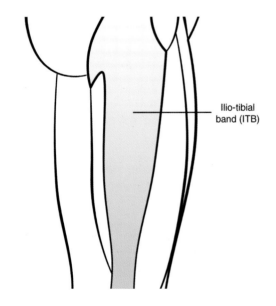

Ilio-tibial band (ITB)

All of these factors result in the ITB tightening and rubbing against skeletal structures, causing inflammation and considerable discomfort.

Symptoms

- Discomfort on the outside of the knee or hip
- A 'clicking' sensation on knee flexion on the outside of the knee as the tendon rubs against the bone
- Pain in the knee or hip when attempting to walk downstairs, and sometimes when sitting down in a low chair
- Sudden onset of pain several kilometres into a run

Treatment

Along with the usual RICE protocol, the best ways to treat ITB syndrome are rest and stretching. If you nip the injury in the bud early on, you can save yourself literally weeks of discomfort as this injury can last for a very long time. If the ITB persists for longer than two weeks, I strongly suggest you seek professional advice.

Blisters

Blisters are a menace for all runners and can be one of the most frustrating injuries you pick up over the course of your training. New shoes and regular training sessions are ideal conditions for blisters to form, as your soft skin is exposed to something it's not used to, and you're at risk of what best resembles a mini water balloon on your foot or toe.

However, there is good news. There are several steps you can take to reduce your chances of getting blisters and, should you get one, there is some simple advice on how to treat it.

The top five blister-busting tips are as follows:

1 Make sure your trainers fit properly: Even if they are just a fraction too small, you are a blister patient waiting to happen.

2 Wear proper socks: Specialist running socks are designed to wick away sweat and prevent rubbing. Cotton socks are a big no-no, so get yourself some decent ones.

3 Use petroleum jelly: A bit of grease goes a long way in preventing rubbing, so apply a little bit on vulnerable areas before a run.

4 To burst or not to burst? If you develop a blister and it's not painful, leave it alone – you could make it worse if you play with it. If it's sore and resembles a small water balloon, use a sterilised needle and press out the fluid (to sterilise a needle, the easiest thing to do is place it in boiling water for 30 seconds). Follow up with some antiseptic cream and a plaster.

5 Cover up: If you need to cover up a blister, use moleskin plasters as they will reduce rubbing on other toes and thus reduce friction. Moleskin plasters are specifically designed for active people as they help to protect soft blistered skin and have a smooth surface to prevent further rubbing.

CANCER RESEARCH UK

START/FINISH

11 race day: the final hurdle

With the best part of 10 weeks of training under your (now smaller) belt, the day of reckoning suddenly arrives – and this is the time when a lot of runners hit the panic button.

What should I eat in the morning? What should I drink? What do I do with my car keys? What shall I wear?

All these questions are common causes of anxiety in the days leading up to a 5k or 10k event, but I hope that this chapter will help to alleviate some of your concerns, so that you can turn up at the start in good time, know that you're well fed and watered, and ready to tackle the course.

❖ wakey wakey! It's been a long night

If your sole aim of taking part in the race is that it is the perfect excuse to raise money for charity and have a good laugh with friends while wearing a crazy costume, then the chances are that you'll be feeling more excited about the race than nervous. However, for those of you who are running it to get under a certain time, then the night before the race can be an unsettled one. The combination of fear of failure and nervous excitement is a perfect recipe for a restless night's sleep and, as a result, very heavy eyes in the morning.

If you find that your good intentions of an early night result in a just a few hours of disturbed sleep, do not panic. You will not be the only runner in this position and, contrary to what you what might think, the lack of sleep will not affect your running performance. With the help of the electric race atmosphere and the adrenaline coursing through your veins, you'll soon forget how badly you slept, and all that fitness you have developed over the past 10–12 weeks will be on hand to help you tackle the 5k or 10k course just as well as if you'd had 10 hours of sleep.

Rise early

No matter how much time you think you'll have to get to the event on the morning of the race, you'll always find that you'll be in a rush. Courtesy of an uncooperative child or the infamous vanishing car keys, time is always a precious commodity, so set the alarm that extra bit early, and give yourself lots of time to eat, drink and relax – and the chance to drive within the speed limit to get to the start on time.

You should always aim to arrive at the site of the event no less than an hour before the gun, so that

Race day fun

Big charity events such as Race for Life have loads of things going on well before the race starts, so don't think that if you turn up too early you'll be bored and left twiddling your thumbs. Although some of the smaller rural events attract slightly less glitz and glamour, there is always something to do and an atmosphere to absorb. With music playing all around and plenty of highly amusing fancy dress costumes to laugh at (maybe yours), why not turn up to the event extra early and soak up the day before your race begins?

you have plenty of time to drop your bags off with friends or at the onsite facilities, have a stretch, visit the bathroom (probably more than once) and soak up the atmosphere.

The gun will not wait for you, so familiarise yourself with the route to the event the night before, allow plenty of time for traffic and start your race day relaxed and calm.

get packing

To buy yourself that extra bit of time in the morning, it's a good idea to pack everything you need for the day of the race the night before. If you leave it until the morning, you're running the risk of rushing it and forgetting to pack something blindingly obvious – such as your running shoes.

To help you out and make sure you don't forget anything important, use the following checklist as you pack, and be safe in the knowledge that you have all the essentials.

Race day kit bag checklist

- Running shoes (if you aren't already wearing them)
- Running number and safety pins
- A bottle of water or sports drink
- A spare top, tracksuit bottoms and a vest/T-shirt
- Tracksuit bottoms
- Sun cream

∵breakfast

Knowing what to eat for breakfast on the morning of the race causes confusion for many runners. When do I eat? How much do I eat? What do I eat?

The key thing to remember when it comes to breakfast is to eat what you are used to and what you know you are able to tolerate. Swapping your usual jam and toast for a bowl of porridge, just because you read somewhere that it's a good pre-race breakfast, could be a disastrous decision if your stomach is unhappy with the introduction of something it's not used to digesting before a race. The runs, stomach cramps and bloating are all symptoms you could experience if you eat something you are intolerant to – not something you need when you're surrounded by hundreds or even thousands of runners and only a dozen or so portaloos!

So, the golden rule of the pre-race breakfast is: stick to what you know.

Provided you have been following a well-balanced diet throughout your training, there is no need to panic about whether you've got enough energy in the tank to see you through the race. If you eat a

carbohydrate-rich meal the night before, this should ensure that you have sufficient carbs on board to see you through the race, so don't feel compelled to shovel down a pasta-sized bowl of muesli or porridge at 7 a.m. on the day of the race.

∵at the venue

Beat the traffic

If the event is in your home town, then the chances are that you'll know the area well enough to get to the course – but don't be complacent. Big events attract a lot of traffic so not only can the roads get gridlocked near the event but often certain roads are closed off as they may be part of the course.

Check your local area website or race day information pack to find out the best route to the venue, where to park and which roads will be closed. If possible, try to walk to the event – it's not as though you're not fit enough, and a good walk is the perfect way to warm up your muscles.

The build-up

Always check your race information pack to see if there is a requirement for you to check in and register your arrival. Most events will already have

---

Butterflies in your tummy

If nerves, apprehension or simply a lack of time are getting the better of you on the morning of the race, and you find it difficult to eat anything, don't panic. This is really common and the very reason why it's a good idea to pack some fruit and snack bars in your kit bag to cater for such eventualities. Munching on these en route to the race venue will be sufficient to raise your blood sugar levels a little, fill your belly and help to alleviate any hunger pangs.

posted you your race number and race chip (if required), so organisers don't always require you to confirm your arrival – but some do, so it's best to get that out of the way and then get ready for the race. Although not available at all races, a race chip is a coin-sized device which accurately times how long it takes you to run the race. You clip it to the laces of your running shoes and special sensors at the start line and finish line pick up your chip's unique code number and time how long it takes you to get round the course.

Avoid temptation

Nearly all events have their fair share of sports nutrition companies giving away or selling their special 'go faster' drink or snack bar to help you through the race, but be very cautious about eating something that you've never eaten before.

It's an issue that has been referred to several times in this book, but an hour before the race is really no time to start tasting new, brightly coloured sweet drinks or snack bars. Chances are they might be fine and not irritate your stomach one bit, but if they do the only place you'll be running is to the loo.

Warming up

As soon as you arrive in the 'holding area' at the venue and start milling around with the other runners, it's a good idea to start some gentle stretches – even if there's still an hour to go before the start.

If the weather is cold, make sure you are wrapped up warm and start stretching gently. At most big events, the organisers usually have a fitness expert up on stage to help get you in the mood and warmed up around 30 minutes before the start, so it's a good idea to join in to make sure you don't miss stretching some of the key muscles.

the final countdown

Once you've stretched, the final 20–30 minutes before the official start of the race can be manic. It seems that the final 30-minute countdown creates panic and causes everyone to rush around like headless chickens trying to put the finishing touches to their race preparation.

A mad dash to the loo for a final pee, dumping clothes and belongings with family and friends, and making a beeline for a place on the start line are just a few of the things that hundreds of people do before the race, so get organised and use the following tips to avoid getting caught up with the crowds.

Final countdown checklist (20–30 minutes before the start)

- Take a pee: Follow all the advice in Chapter 8 on hydration and avoid drinking too much. Once you have passed the 'pee test', stop drinking and you'll find you won't need to queue for the toilets in the dying minutes before the gun fires.

- Check your shoelaces: Make sure your laces are tied tight (but not too tight) and are double bowed. Undone laces are a hazard to yourself and other runners so make sure they are tied properly.

- Strip: If it's a cool day and you're wearing over-clothes to keep warm, now is the time to take them off and leave them in the designated area or with family and friends. Keep moving to stay warm.

- Take your place: Get ready. Even if you think 20 minutes before the race is due to start is ages away, after a natter with fellow runners and a few last-minute stretches, time will fly by and you'll be good to go before you know it. Get ready for that call to make your way to the start line.

bang! The race is on ...

A time for reflection

Before you know it, the start of the race is under way, and this is where all those weeks of training will come to fruition.

For many runners, the start of the race is the climax of a long and hard journey to running fitness – and the realisation that just weeks ago you could barely run for a bus and now you are about to run 5k or 10k is a moment to cherish. As you take those first intrepid steps of the race, look back on what you have achieved and aim to thoroughly enjoy what you are about to do.

Equally, even for runners who haven't found the training particularly difficult, the start of a Race for Life event is often a time for reflection on the memory of a loved one who has lost their battle with cancer. So many emotional thoughts flood runners' minds when they start a race that it can be a very special moment.

Cherish it and relish it but, above all, enjoy it!

Easy does it

With all these emotions flooding your mind and a surge of adrenaline coursing through your veins, it's really easy to find yourself shooting off at lightning-quick pace as nervous excitement gets the better of you. Of course, at large events you may find yourself not going anywhere very fast at the beginning due to the sheer volume of runners bunched around you, but if you find yourself in space, be careful not to set off too quickly and end up exhausting yourself before you've even reached the halfway point.

If you are aiming for a specific time, making sure you don't 'over-pace' is essential, as all those weeks of training could be wasted if you deplete your energy stores in the first kilometre or two. Joe McAlister, Irish half marathon champion and Irish 10k silver medallist, is famous for saying, 'You can't win the race in the first mile, but you can lose it by going out too hard' – something worth keeping in mind when the gun goes.

'As a cancer sufferer, I have found running to be a fantastic release. Training with friends for Race for Life events has been such good fun and I would recommend anyone to take part in at least one event.'

Elizabeth Ganapathy

Enjoy the experience

Once you're through the hustle and bustle of the start, and you get into your running rhythm, don't forget to enjoy yourself. Whatever background you have come from and whatever reason you have for running – be it to lose weight, raise money for charity or break a personal best – I cannot stress highly enough the importance of making the most of the day and enjoying what you are doing.

Your training for the past few months may have been tough, insufficient or, dare I say it, virtually non-existent, but cherishing any event is essential to get the most out of it and give you the inspiration to maybe even try it again. Naturally, your enjoyment

may only come at the end when you have succeeded in your goal to finish the course without walking, or you finish in a good time, but do not let a failure to achieve these goals take away the enjoyment and sense of occasion of the day. If you miss out on your goal, don't worry – there is always next time.

There are hundreds of 5k and 10k events in the UK and around the world so if you missed out on finishing under a certain time, or the desire to walk overcame you with only a few hundred yards left, take comfort in the knowledge that there will be another race near you soon – and there could be a place in it with your name on.

Case study

Name: Caron Williamson

Age: 33

Occupation: Mum and Business Consultant

Years of running experience: Seven

The hardest thing, in my experience, is pacing yourself from the start. There are usually lots of runners milling around and once you start moving the temptation is to launch into a full sprint. A mixture of nerves and adrenaline seem to propel you forward much quicker than you would normally be capable of in training. The key is to slow yourself down enough so that you hit a comfortable pace which you can maintain for the whole distance.

Once you are up and running it can be a little disconcerting when people keep overtaking you. It can impact your motivation, if you let it. I find it helpful to fix my eyes on somebody already in front of me, who is going more or less at my pace. Then you can either keep your eyes on them as a distraction technique when the going gets tough, or, if you are feeling good, try to overtake them. Don't worry if they disappear at pace into the distance – simply select another runner and apply the same technique!

I find the hardest part in any run is around the middle point. At this point I start to feel quite tired and yet the end of the race still feels very far away. Things that have helped me to get through this are little mental tricks, like counting your footsteps up to eight or singing a song you like in your head. When I had my baby I used these same tricks while I was in labour! It's amazing how distracting yourself can take you through pain and out on to the other side.

Then before you know it you are close enough to the end to start enjoying it, maybe even speed up a little. Thanks to the adrenaline and training your time should hopefully come as a nice surprise!

12 summary and frequently asked questions

Irrespective of whether you come to this chapter at the beginning, middle or end of your training, the chances are that running is (or will very soon be) very much part of your life.

Even if you thought years or even months ago that there was more chance of pigs flying than you seeing the day you looked forward to a gentle 20-minute jog, it's amazing how such a simple activity can grip you and give you such a feel-good factor.

The beauty of the hundreds of 5k and 10k events which take place up and down the country is that there is such a diverse range of races and there is always one that will catch your eye – even if you think you'll only ever do one event. If I had a penny for every time I heard an exhausted runner say 'never again' after a race, only to start looking for another one to run a few weeks later, I'd be a very wealthy man.

With such a range of events to choose from, the temptation to try out your new found fitness on a hilly 5k course or a fast urban 10k is alluring to most people who have caught the running bug, so don't think you won't be seduced sooner or later.

knowledge is power

As you will have noticed, the information in this book has been written specifically for people who are either new to the world of jogging with little or no idea of how to prepare for a 5k or 10k race, or for those who have been jogging recreationally for a bit and need a little help to go on to the next level.

Every chapter has given you everything you need to know to get started in this crazy world of running and help provide you with the knowledge you need to prepare your novice running legs to carry you around a 5k or 10k course with relative ease – provided you actually do the training of course.

For many of you who hope to keep running, but have no desire to run a 5k or 10k any faster, this book will hopefully continue to serve you well for many years to come and will help answer any injury, nutrition or training questions you may have in your future running years; but for the competitive among you, delving deeper into the science of running may very well come in handy.

Wherever your interest lies, be it in the training aspect of running or what food to eat for improving sporting performance, there are hundreds of publications available on both the bookshelves on the high street and the virtual shelves on the internet.

A vast array of books have been written by a vast array of 'experts' all with their own unique training or eating philosophies, which claim to 'guarantee' that a certain training method or specific eating regime will help to shave minutes off your PB or help give you the endurance of the Duracell bunny.

Over the years, for both my own interest and research, I have read a lot of books by a lot of experts, most with far more knowledge of the human body than me. As intriguing and interesting as most of these books are, I have learnt one very valuable lesson which runners of any ability should note when searching for the 'ultimate running / nutrition plan'.

The old adage 'one man's meat is another man's poison' could not be more true when it comes to different training methods and nutrition pro-grammes, and is something every runner should bear in mind when reading new material or trying out new training theories or nutritional plans.

One of a kind

Active or sedentary, we are all so different in so many ways.

Autopsies of the human body over the years have shown huge variations in the size of our livers, kidneys, hearts and skeletal musculature, clearly demonstrating that we are all unique.

As a result of our individual diversity, we must accept that applying a 'one size fits all' philosophy when it comes to training, eating or even medicating is naïve and possibly even dangerous in some instances.

The subject of biochemical individuality is clearly beyond the scope of this book, but it's something you should certainly keep in mind when exploring other books and adopting new training regimes.

Not for one moment am I suggesting you steer clear of any new radical training philosophy you read about, all I recommend is that you always listen to your body and if something doesn't feel right or you frequently feel unwell after a training session or a new way of eating, I suggest you stop immediately and review what you are doing.

Certain training principles outlined in some (often controversial) books may very well work wonders for some runners and help you to achieve incredible

Must-reads for ambitious runners

There are many great books out there that will serve you very well on your bedside table, but there are three books I strongly recommend buying to help you learn about the running body.

Lore of Running **(Human Kinetics Europe)**
Written by Tim Noakes MD, who is both a professor of exercise and sports science and an accomplished runner. This book is an excellent read and will keep you motivated for years. It is full of fascinating training principles and covers every aspect of running you could wish for.

Born to Run **(Profile Books)**
Written by Christopher McDougall, who gives a compelling insight into the world of running. A real page turner and a book so inspirational you'll want to get up and go for a run as soon as you've finished every chapter.

The Complete Guide to Sports Nutrition **(A&C Black)**
Written by leading nutritionist Anita Bean, this book has sold thousands of copies worldwide and is as close to a bible on sports nutrition as you could possibly get. Packed full of valuable information on how to eat for performance, hydration and key supplements, this book should be kept close to hand at all times.

leaps in running fitness, but they may equally not suit your biochemistry and actually have a detrimental effect on you.

∴frequently asked questions

As any personal trainer, nutritionist or physiotherapist will tell you, there are some questions which keep cropping up time and time again from interested clients who crave to understand more about their training regime, diet plan or injury. No doubt, at some stage during your training there will be times when you'll be dying to know the answer to a question but had no one to ask other than good old Google – from which the answers are often somewhat questionable.

So, to help answer some of the most common questions I have been asked over the years from runners taking part in 5k and 10k races, here is a list of the top ten.

1. I was told by a friend that running is bad for your joints. Is this true?

Nearly every client I have trained for a 5k or 10k race has expressed a degree of concern that they will do irreparable damage to their joints from the regular pounding that they are exposed to while running. This concern is invariably made worse by (usually jealous or lazy) friends who say categorically that running ruins the knees and you should stop immediately and take up swimming or golf.

Let's get this into perspective. If our joints are so badly and highly susceptible to injury, why are there still hundreds of thousands of men and women well into their retirement years, still running on a regular basis?

The view that running is going to cripple us and make us require a new pair of hips or knees in our retirement years is not only grossly inaccurate but in fact the complete opposite of the truth. It is a proven scientific fact that weight-bearing exercise such as running, done in moderation, actually helps to keep bones strong, thereby reducing our chances of becoming crippled later on in life.

Of course, for the small extreme section of the running community who live their lives for running and regularly cover in excess of 70 miles a week, I would certainly support the theory that this excessive road running could to lead to joint problems in the future, but it's by no means a certainty. As with everything in life, anything in moderation, is unlikely to do you harm. Take it to extremes, however, and you are tempting fate.

Whether you are a casual runner, or plan to run in 5k or 10k races regularly, there is no reason why your joints should pose any problems, now or at any time in the future. Naturally, the unlucky few with a genetic predisposition for weak joints might be forced to end their running careers prematurely, but for the majority of people, there is no reason why running cannot be enjoyed pain-free, right into your 50s, 60s,70s or 80s.

2. Why does my heart rate keep rising when I'm running on the flat and at an even pace?

Understanding the complex physiology of how the heart responds to exercise is something some fitness enthusiasts obsess about, but for most people a basic understanding of why the heart does what it does during exercise is sufficient.

However, one issue that confuses many people is the gradual increase in heart rate that occurs during a run, despite keeping the pace constant. Undulations in the surface may be partly responsible but even if you were to run on a treadmill at a constant pace and at the same speed and incline for an hour or so, you would find that your heart rate slowly creeps up. This is a process known as cardiovascular drift and it is perfectly normal.

Although there are a number of explanations as to why your heart rate gradually increases, the dehydrating effects of training has been found to be the most likely cause. With blood being diverted to the skin to keep the body cool, less blood is available for the heart to pump around the body. As a result, the heart must beat more quickly to keep the working muscles supplied with sufficient amounts of oxygenated blood. Although this theory is still inconclusive, it certainly seems to be the most likely explanation. As dramatic as all this sounds, cardio-vascular drift is perfectly normal, so there's no need to be worried if any of this sounds familiar. However, if you see regular major fluctuations in heart rate during training, a trip to the doctor is strongly advised.

3. Is the nutritional supplement glucosamine a good supplement to take during my running training?

The popularity of glucosamine has increased substantially over the years so much so that it is even held in high regard by many GPs. That glucosamine is now recognised to be an effective treatment for joints within orthodox medicine is very significant.

However, effective as glucosamine is, very few people actually understand what it is or how it works. What many people are unaware of is that it is actually already manufactured by the body, although as we get older our body becomes less efficient at producing it. Glucosamine can help with joint problems for two reasons.

First, it stimulates the manufacture of things called glycosaminoglycans, which are important components of cartilage. Second, it helps with the incorporation of sulphur into the cartilage – hence the reason why glucosamine sulphate is generally regarded to be the best form of the supplement.

Glucosamine is effective at manufacturing new cartilage and over time it will help to reduce arthritic pain, so if you fit into this category it might be worth considering a consultation with your GP. However, be aware that it will do nothing to help you if you have sore knees or joints in general. Glucosamine sulphate or similar supplements are not painkillers or miracle cures; they simply help to stimulate the body to grow more cartilage.

Lastly, it is worth being extra cautious if you are thinking of taking glucosamine and you are taking blood thinning medication such as warfarin. There is some evidence to suggest that combining the two could lead to an increased risk of bleeding. If in doubt, consult your GP.

4. Why do I get a stitch?

The runner's stitch, which usually manifests itself in the lower abdomen just below the ribs in the middle or the right-hand side, is perhaps one of the most common and frustrating ailments experienced by runners of all abilities – from novices right through to those who think nothing of a gentle 10 mile run before breakfast. What makes the stitch an even more infuriating pain is that we are still not 100 per cent sure what causes it.

Theories ranging from an overstretched stomach ligament to trapped wind have all been put forward by physiologists, but still no one is sure why they can come on without any particular reason and why it can sometimes cause referred pain in the shoulder. Although there is evidence to suggest that a spasm of the diaphragm is closely linked to the two sites of discomfort, we still don't know for sure, so research continues. There are a number of precautions you can take to significantly reduce your chances of getting a stitch.

Ways to avoid getting stitches

- **Avoid food and water 2–3 hours before exercise:** This could help by reducing the load on your stomach and limit any ligament stretching.

- **Avoid downhill running where possible:** Although it is of course not easy, especially if you live in a hilly area, try to avoid running for long periods down steep hills as this jolting motion appears to bring on the symptoms of a stitch. If you do run downhill, try and run as smoothly as you can and avoid sending shock waves through your legs and up into your body.

  - **Go easy:** A lot of people find that stitches can be brought on by setting off for a run too fast, so always make sure you have a good warm up before you take on your training run and ease yourself into it gently.

  - **Learn to breathe:** Although you'd be forgiven for thinking that seeing that you've made it to 30, 40 or 50 years old and you're reading this, you may have mastered this skill, it doesn't necessarily mean that you have learnt how to do it properly. It has been proven that learning to breathe 'diaphragmatically' or 'belly

breathe', as opposed to relying purely on the chest muscles to draw in air, significantly helps to reduce instances of stitches. The reasons for this are varied and too complex to go into detail in this book, but learning proper breathing techniques can help you banish the dreaded stitch forever. To learn how to breathe diaphragmatically, the best way is to simply lie on the floor and position a large object, such as a book, on your stomach. All you need to do next is to make sure that when you breathe in the book should rise and when you breathe out, the book should descend. This movement indicates that you are 'belly breathing' and with practice, it will become natural to breathe this way during a run and therefore banish the dreaded stitch.

- **Do those stomach strengtheners:** Interestingly, there is evidence to suggest that keeping your stomach muscles strong is a great way to avoid being susceptible to stitches. By performing a series of abdominal strengthening exercises a few times a week is all it takes to keep your core strong and avoid that annoying stabbing pain in your side. The stomach strengthening exercises in chapter 7 are a great place to start.

- **Visit the bathroom:** Making sure both your bladder and bowels are empty before a run are also good measures to avoid a stitch. The exact reasons are not clearly understood but a quick visit to the bathroom is strongly advised. As effective as all these measures are, they are sadly no use it you are just 10 minutes into a run and the dreaded stitch strikes, causing you to ease your pace or even stop. The good news is that there are a few things you can do to calm down the discomfort and help you finish your run without being in pain.

The best remedy for alleviating a stitch is to slow your jogging pace right down, lean forwards slightly and breathe through pursed lips. This *forced exhalation* is believed to help calm the diaphragm down and help disperse the stitch pain in the abdomen.

5. Is it possible to be too overweight to run?

This is a really common question and one which, to a degree, you must answer yourself. If you have been inactive for a few years or have been unable to find the time to run due to family commitments, you may feel you have put on a few pounds which you'd now quite like to lose.

Seeing that running is one of the best forms of activity you can do to improve cardiovascular fitness, strengthen the heart and lose weight it is an obvious choice for many people who want to lose a few pounds, but often there is a degree of reluctance to begin jogging over concerns that it might actually do more harm than good, especially if you are very overweight.

Firstly, the most important thing you must do, as mentioned at the beginning of the book, is to make an appointment with your GP to make sure your blood pressure is within normal limits and to give you piece of mind that your doctor cannot see any medical reason why you should not start a gentle jogging regime.

Secondly, you must *always* make sure you start very gently and not be afraid to include plenty of walking breaks for the benefit of your heart and your joints. If you are carrying excess weight and your heart and joints are not used to the stress which jogging places on them, there is a chance that you could do yourself harm or damage your joints. Every part of your body, from your heart to your back to your hips, is going to need time to adjust to the demands that a jogging regime asks and if you ask too much of them too soon you are likely to end up with an injury.

The best piece of advice I offer anyone who is overweight and wants to start jogging is to only head out for 10–15 minutes for the first two weeks or so and begin your regime with a split between walking and light jogging. For example, if you are able to then jog for one minute, follow it up with at least one minute of walking – longer if you feel you need more time. Never feel pressured to jog any further than you feel comfortable.

6. Why do I feel so lethargic and lacklustre?

In a world which feels like it is moving at 100mph, courtesy of the time we are expected to spend at work combined with the time we want to spend with our family, it is rare that we get anywhere near the eight hours sleep we should be getting.

Add in a training regime for a 5k and 10k run at the beginning or end of the day and all of a sudden your daily routine is even more hectic and very quickly everything can feel like it's too much and you find yourself utterly exhausted.

Although regular exercise has been proven to help boost energy levels and should in fact help to invigorate your well-being, if you are not getting enough sleep then fatigue can easily accumulate and creep up on you without you really noticing.

So, if you are finding your weekly runs a little tougher than you think they should be, sit back and evaluate your weekly routine and see how many hours of sleep you are getting per night. If you notice it is averaging closer to six hours than eight hours then there is every chance you've found a reason for your lethargy. It might not be easy, but try and be disciplined and take yourself off to bed an hour or so earlier every night. You'll be amazed how much difference just an extra hour of sleep per night can make, so for the good of your training and general well-being try and address your lack of sleep.

However, if you feel you are getting plenty of sleep yet still feel a little lacklustre, lethargic and generally fatigued, it might be worth getting your iron levels looked at. Iron is a vital mineral in helping the body to transport oxygen around the body. Without it, the blood would not be able to supply the muscles with sufficient oxygen to be able to work effectively.

A lack of iron in the blood (anaemia) is not that uncommon, especially in women, even in those not training for a 5k or 10k race. If you do feel uncharacteristically fatigued and lethargic, have a look under your eyelids and note their colour. If they are pale, it would pay to see your doctor who will be able to check your iron levels.

Iron can be found in all meat products, especially red meat, along with green leafy vegetables, pulses and apricots. Vegetarians should keep a look out for signs of anaemia, as iron from plant foods is not as easily absorbed as that from meat. In addition, seemingly innocent drinks such as tea and coffee can inhibit the absorption of iron into the blood stream, so try to make sure you consume plenty of vitamin C rich foods or drinks (such as orange or cranberry juice) to help enhance iron absorption. The need for iron supplementation is not always necessary. A well-balanced diet should provide you with enough iron to meet the demands of training. If you supplement your diet with extra iron when you already have sufficient

stores, it can create a range of health problems from frequent infections to an increased risk of heart disease, if taken for long periods of time.

7. Who should I see first if I have an injury – my GP or an alternative practitioner?

It's not easy to answer this question honestly without sounding a little controversial, but taking a trip to your overworked doctor is not always the best option to have a running injury diagnosed or treated. GPs have an incredible amount of knowledge about many medical ailments but unless they have a particular interest in the field, their diagnosis and suggested treatment for many soft tissue injuries is nowhere near as good as a sports injury expert such as a physiotherapist.

Doctors are strapped for resources and time and not for one minute would I or any sports injury specialist expect them to be an expert in every field. Interestingly, a GP and friend of mine discussed this issue at length. Not only does he agree with the general lack of sporting injury knowledge of most of his colleagues, but he summed it up by saying, 'GPs know not a lot about a lot and consultants, physiotherapists, etc. know a lot about not a lot'.

The days when a doctor was the only person who knew anything and everything about illness and injury are well behind us. Physiotherapists, dieticians, osteopaths and sports therapists are all well established, regulated and can provide effective forms of treatment that will not only help to take the pressure off the overworked GP, but will also provide a specialist practitioner for specific ailments.

If you have an injury and don't want to spend the money consulting a private therapist, my advice would be to take a trip to your GP if you feel the injury is bad enough and ask for a referral to an NHS physiotherapist.

If money isn't a problem, go straight to a specialist who will have seen your injury hundreds of times before and begin the correct treatment immediately. Finding a good physiotherapist can be tricky, so ask friends if they know of a good one or ask your GP. Always make sure they are a charted physiotherapist with the appropriate qualifications. If in doubt, contact The Chartered Society of Physiotherapy at www.ccp.org.uk who will put you in touch with a suitable practitioner.

Without doubt, doctors are lifesavers and have an incredibly difficult job to do with limited time and resources. Many would not profess to know a lot about sports medicine so why bother them just because they are 'free'? If you want the right treatment, you've got to seek the right professional.

8. Is a bag of frozen peas or a hot water bottle best if I have an injury?

This is a really common question and one that is really important to get right. The trouble is, most people choose the wrong option when deciding on whether to opt for hot or cold, invariably making the injury worse rather than better.

When you damage soft tissue and inflammation occurs, it is essential that you treat the area immediately and reduce the inflammation. In cases of torn muscles, tiny little blood vessels within the muscle tissue are also torn, making your choice of hot or cold even more important. Choose the wrong one and you'll attract blood to the area rather than divert it, so which one is it?

The answer is frozen peas every time as part of the well known RICE procedure – Rest, Ice, Compression and Elevation (of the injury). By applying cold to the area, you constrict the tiny blood capillaries and reduce the flow of blood to the area, thereby reducing the inflammatory response. By applying a hot water bottle, you will do the exact opposite and dilate the capillaries causing a gush of blood to the area and making the injury far worse.

The only time you can start thinking about applying heat in the form of a water bottle or hot bath is when all the inflammation, pain (and any swelling) has gone.

9. Is it ok if I do most of my training on a treadmill?

Treadmills are great pieces of equipment abundant in every gym up and down the country. Although some people (and especially running purists) hate the idea of running in a muggy gym, when the wilderness outside has far more to offer, some feel comforted by the knowledge that if fatigue sets in and the legs refuse to work anymore, they can just hop off and head for the shower, rather than be 3 miles or so away from home.

Whatever your opinion on treadmills, there is little doubt that they do have a positive role to play in your preparations for a 5k or 10k race. Just some of the advantages include:

- the ability to adjust your running pace at the push of a button;
- the ability to increase the incline of your run at any time to push yourself a little harder;
- having your water bottle close at hand – not in your hand;
- having a TV to watch while running, which can help to pass the time;
- having peace of mind that if you get a niggle or you get tired, you can hop off whenever you like and call it a day.

As wonderful as they may sound, treadmills do have several disadvantages. Other than the risk of putting a foot out of place and comically (and embarrassingly)

falling off the machine, the main disadvantage is that the surface you run on while on the treadmill does not accurately simulate the surface you will be running on for the other training runs or the race itself. Although this may not sound like a major problem, it can become one if you spend too much time on the treadmill rather than outside on the roads. The soft treadmill runway will not prepare your muscles and joints effectively for running on the harder surfaces and making the transition from jogging 5k on a soft treadmill to a hard road can lead to injury.

Tip

Whenever you do a run on the treadmill, set the incline to at least 1 per cent. This helps to mimic road running a little better than running on a 0 per cent incline.

By all means use the treadmill every now and again to complement outdoor training, but try and resist the temptation to over rely on it.

10. Which side of the road should I run on if there is no pavement?

Running on the road rather than the pavement is obviously a dangerous practice and should be avoided wherever possible.

We are all too aware of the number of nutters there are behind the wheel these days and all it takes is a runner being in the wrong place at the wrong time and a serious accident is all too likely.

However, there are times when jogging on a road, albeit for a short time, is unavoidable, and for safety reasons it is essential that you choose to run on the correct side of the road – which is on the side of oncoming traffic.

It is far safer for you to run in a direction where you can see oncoming vehicles so that you can give yourself plenty of time to hop up onto an embankment if the oncoming vehicle fails to see you.

There is an exception to the rule though. If you are jogging on the road and see an upcoming right-hand corner (assuming you are running in the UK on the right-hand side of the road), it is advisable that you cross over the road in good time so that you are not faced with a car suddenly appearing around the corner. They will not see you and you will not see them, so for safety reasons, cross to the other side so that you give drivers and yourself plenty of time to be aware of each other's presence.

Running on the road is dangerous and should be avoided at all costs, but if you must, make sure you are wearing a high visibility top and *never* use an iPod or MP3 player. You will need all your senses about you, and other than your eyes, your ears are the best sense you have when jogging on the road.

13 now you've got the running bug: taking it further

There is every chance that now you have finished your 5k or 10k race you never want to see a pair of running shoes again. For some people, for a number of reasons ranging from ill health, injuries or simply a lack of time, the weeks of training and the race itself were not as enjoyable as they thought they would be and the mere thought of going through it all again fills them with dread.

Thankfully, in my experience, these cases are rare and the overwhelming majority of people are itching to sign up for another race and keep their running fitness going. Despite the fact that we all have hectic lives and feel as though there are not enough hours in the day to do what we want, there is always time to squeeze in at least two or three short runs in even the busiest of weeks.

∴ running – your natural and legal high

Even if the first time you ran was when you began your training for your 5k or 10k race, you would have seen and felt the positive impact that regular jogging had on your waistline, state of mind and energy levels.

In a world where pharmaceutical drugs are often prescribed too readily and unnecessarily, running is without doubt (and with a plethora of scientific evidence to back it up) one of the most potent and broad spectrum natural remedies you can 'take' to address a selection of physical and mental conditions.

Regular running is known to release natural 'pain-killing' chemicals called endorphins into the blood stream, which is produced when we exercise on a regular basis. Endorphins make us feel fantastic and are one of the main reasons why running can be so addictive and leaves us in that euphoric high which most runners get after a training run.

It is precisely this 'feel good factor' that comes from endorphins, making us feel amazing and thereby encouraging us to continue our love affair with running – sometimes with extreme consequences.

⁘going the extra mile – or 26

If you gave your 5k or 10k race everything you've got and collapsed in a sweaty heap after you crossed the finish line, the last thing on your mind will be signing up for your next running challenge. With a racing heart and legs like jelly, a drink, a shower and the sofa are the only things you really look forward to, but as time goes on this can all change.

If you have well and truly caught the running bug and are eager to get a taste of what more the world of running has to offer you, then you need look no further than the challenge of a half or full marathon.

The half marathon – 13.1 miles (21.1 kilometres)

It might be just over twice as far as a 10k but the half marathon, for many, is a distance which offers the perfect balance between being a tough, but at the same time realistic, challenge.

As with all running events, half marathons in particular are more popular now than they have ever been. With the UK hosting Europe's largest half marathon event in the shape of the Great North Run, there are dozens of mass participation (and small participation) half marathons you can enter.

Although the thought of running a half marathon, which is effectively running a 10k race – and then turning around and doing it again, sounds like a mission impossible, it may surprise you that it is not nearly as hard as you might think.

How to prepare

The training for a half marathon, although more time consuming, is simply just an extension of the training you have done for your 5k or 10k race. The long runs which you have been doing on a Saturday or Sunday, which reached a maximum distance of 5–11k (or 30–60 minutes) are simply built on over the weeks, and over time, your body naturally adapts to the extra work being asked of it.

Provided you give yourself enough time to get in shape, the training for a 13.1-mile run is far more within your ability than you might think. With a supportive family, who will need to live without you for a few hours every week, and a determined mind-set to focus on the volume of training you'll need to do, a half marathon is well within your means – the key ingredient needed is the desire to do it. Whether your motivation is to raise money for charity or to prove to yourself you have got what it takes to take on a challenge and overcome it, you need to have passion and true desire if you are to cross that finish line after running 13.1 miles.

A half marathon is the ideal distance to consider taking after your 10k race, so if you are interested, why not look into signing up for one of the following races:

- The Great North Run
- Bristol Half Marathon
- Reading Half Marathon
- Cardiff Half Marathon
- Bath Half Marathon

The marathon – 26.2 miles (42.2 kilometres)

If you're looking for the ultimate challenge and have a burning desire to really see if you've got the drive and determination to compete in one of the toughest

running events known to man, then look no further than the marathon.

26.2 miles or 42.2 kilometres is a long way in your car, let alone on your feet, so you have to be 100 per cent committed to it before you decide to sign up to an event.

As crazy as the notion of running 42 kilometres might sound to non-runners and even regular runners, there is clearly something very seductive about the event which is luring record numbers of people to take on the challenge.

Back in 1981, when the London marathon was first organised, there were just 20,000 applicants. Jump forward to 2010 and a staggering 162,000 people applied to take part in the event with a record number of 51,266 runners being accepted to run.

How to prepare

The marathon is the ultimate challenge for anyone wanting to put themselves through a gruelling 5–6 month training regime and push the boundaries of their mental and physical resilience.

The physical aspect of training for the race is, again, in essence an extension of your training for a 5k, 10k, or half marathon. The time and miles you put in on the road just keep getting longer as you encourage your body to adapt to working for anything up to five hours. Weekly training distances of 40–50 miles are generally regarded to be the 'norm' in the latter stages of marathon training, with many top runners exceeding this by up to three times in cases.

Like the half marathon, the key to marathon success is to have an incredibly determined, even stubborn, mindset to take the challenge head on and recognise that the long months of training, let alone the race, will push you to your limits.

The journey of a marathon runner from his/her very first training run to the final step of the race, is a roller coaster ride of emotions – this can be helped

if they are kept in check by supportive friends and family. A focused mindset is essential but you'll be hard pushed to find a marathon finisher who doesn't credit his/her family and friends for their support and a shoulder to cry on when the going gets tough.

Despite the overwhelming challenge that the marathon presents, the statistics prove to you that it is an event that runners of all abilities (even absolute beginners) are drawn to and can't resist taking on. It might seem crazy to some people but having run a marathon or two myself, I can honestly say it was the best thing I have ever done. I may have wobbled both physically and mentally along the way and put a huge amount of pressure on myself to run it quickly, but I still look back fondly on the day of my first marathon and am so glad I did it.

Even if you only ever anticipate running one marathon in your lifetime and swear you'll never do another one, I can guarantee you'll never regret it. You would have done what just 1 per cent of the population have done and the overwhelming feeling of satisfaction, achievement and fulfilment will stay with you for the rest of your life.

Why not look into signing up for one of these great marathons:

- The Virgin London Marathon
- The New York Marathon
- The Edinburgh Marathon
- The Berlin Marathon
- The Paris Marathon

respect the challenge

As you will know by now, the training for your 5k and 10k race is far from easy. Finding the time to manage your everyday life with your three or even four weekly training runs is not easy – and I'm afraid it only gets tougher when you commit yourself to a half or full marathon. The sheer volume of running that is required to meet the physical demands of the race mean that the amount of time you need to dedicate to training is increased twofold or threefold. As a result, you have be absolutely sure that your diary is able to cope with regular 'must do' entries, reading along the lines of '90 minute run' or 'run 15 miles non-stop'.

There is no worse feeling than committing to one of these tough distances with every intention of taking the training seriously, and then realising that it is simply impossible to find the time to run. There are so many reasons beyond your control which may make your good intentions impossible to fulfil, leaving you disheartened and frustrated. Studying for exams, overseas business trips or even a new job are all predicaments which may take precedence over regular training, so try and make sure (as far as possible) that the next six months or so of your diary are free enough for you to find time to run. If not, there's always next year.

Lastly, there is the important aspect of the training and the extra nutritional and physiological demands which are placed on the body. Without knowing what types of food, drink and stretching regimes are required to keep the body conditioned to endure the longer running distances, your training could be more challenging that it need be.

Therefore, I'd strongly recommend that you look into buying my other book on how to prepare for half and full marathon distances. *The Marathon and Half Marathon: A Training Guide* (The Crowood Press) is available from all good book stores and covers everything you need to know from the nutritional aspect to the training itself and how to best go about tackling your first half or full marathon.

the top ten UK events

With hundreds of 5k and 10k events held in the UK every year, you are truly spoilt for choice on which to enter. From mass-participation events such as the Cancer Research UK Race for Life series which covers both 5k and 10k distances, to locally organised events in the countryside, you can choose an event that floats your boat, and you're guaranteed to enjoy every last step of it.

Naturally, for practical reasons, most people will choose and enter an event close to where they live to save the time and hassle of travel and accommodation, but sometimes going a little further afield to experience large-scale events with that extra touch of pizzazz is worth the trip. Take friends and family and make a weekend of it – you never know, they might join in next year.

the top five 5k events

1. Race for Life

www.raceforlife.org

With over 230 Race for Life events held throughout the spring and summer months, there is always a venue close by that will be hosting this enormously popular race in aid of Cancer Research UK. Whichever venue you choose, you're guaranteed to have a ball, but to make it extra special why not run at the venue where it all started?

In 1994, the first Race for Life was held in Battersea Park, with only 680 women taking part yet raising an impressive £36,000 in sponsorship. Fast forward 15 years to 2010 and the 230 venues for the event now host over 690,000 runners, raising over £60 million.

Where? Various locations throughout the UK

When? May–July

'As a busy mum, I have found that running is the best activity to do to stay fit as it's free, you can do it anywhere and you feel so good afterwards. I have always found that to help keep motivated, it's a good idea to book a place in a race early on, so that you have a specific goal to aim for.'

Tona Pooley and her niece Emily

How many runners? Several hundred thousand

Why? The race day atmosphere is always amazing at any Race for Life event. The Race for Life Glasgow is one of the largest events held outside London – the razzmatazz is everywhere and it's an event well worth doing if you're up for the challenge.

2. The Big Fun Run

www.bigfunrun.com

The Big Fun Runs are a growing series of 24 Fun Runs staged across the UK. The popularity of these events is growing rapidly and like Race for Life, are ideal events to enter if you are new to running and are after a fun race to take part in.

Where? All over the UK, from Aberdeen to Southampton

When? Summer through to autumn

How many runners? Up to 1,000 runners per event

Why? A fun and light hearted atmosphere at all events making them ideal for new and novice runners.

3. The adidas Women's 5k Challenge

www.womenschallenge.co.uk

With several international athletes taking part in this event every year, there is slightly more emphasis

on this event being more competitive than its Race for Life counterpart, but there is still very much a sense of fun for anyone just wanting to take part in a 5k and raise money for charity.

Where? Hyde Park, London W8 4BQ

When? Usually September

How many runners? 25,000

Why? A big event in central London with a carnival atmosphere – why not?

4. Pants in the Park

www.pantsinthepark.org

At the time of writing, this event is still very much in its infancy, but it certainly looks to be one that will match the fun that has made Race for Life events so popular. It is the brainchild of the chief executive of Prostate UK, who felt that nothing would get more attention than runners wearing decorated Superman-style pants outside their running clothes.

Where? Numerous locations up and down the country, from Belfast to London

When? Usually July

How many runners? Several hundred and growing

Why? It's the perfect opportunity for men (and women) of all ages, shapes and sizes to live out their childhood fantasy and wear highly coloured pants outside their tight Lycra running trousers and pretend they are Superman. Need I say more?

5. Santa Dash 5k: Liverpool

www.santadash.co.uk

Not all 5k and 10k races are held in the summer, and the Liverpool Santa Dash is one of them. Events encouraging runners to wear Santa outfits have grown massively in recent years and this gem in Liverpool is the perfect event to burn off a few mince pies and get into the Christmas spirit.

Where? Liverpool

When? Late November/early December

How many runners? 6,000–7,000

Why? The perfect chance to run with 6,000 other Santas and help you get into a festive mood.

⁛the top five 10k events

There are literally hundreds of 10k running events held nationwide and the number is growing. Although the prospect of running 10k to new runners might seem a little daunting, a 10k (6.2 miles) race is the perfect distance to both challenge your physical fitness and mental toughness. As your fitness levels keep improving, it won't be long before the challenge is not just getting round the course but getting there faster than the last time.

Here are a few of the top 10ks in the country.

1. The Bupa London 10,000

www.london10000.co.uk

Run in the heart of London, the Bupa London 10,000 is the Virgin London Marathon's baby brother – in distance, not in character. A fantastic event for runners of all abilities, it offers a great chance to take in some of the best sights in London while pounding 10k of its finest streets.

Where? Hyde Park Corner, London SW1X 7TA

When? July

How many runners? 20,000

Why? If you don't think you've got the legs to do the London Marathon, this is certainly the next best thing.

2. The Bupa Great Manchester Run

www.greatrun.org

The events in the Great Run series have fast become some of the UK's must-do races. They are all incredibly well organised and cater for runners of all abilities.

Where? Manchester City Centre

When? May

How many runners? 36,000

Why? As one of the fastest-growing 10k events in the country, every year this race just keeps getting better and better.

3. The Bupa Great Edinburgh Run

www.greatrun.org

Scotland's answer to the Bupa London 10,000 (see page 151), the Great Edinburgh Run is a stunning course and takes in many of the Scottish capital's famous landmarks.

Where? Holyrood Park, Edinburgh, Scotland

When? May

How many runners? 10,000

Why? There is no better way to see the Scottish capital up close and personal. Open-top buses just don't cut the mustard.

4. The Brooks Brighton 10k

www.brooksbrighton10k.co.uk

Sometimes, you just want to get out of the city and take in some fresh coastal air to revitalise the lungs, and The Brooks Brighton 10k helps you do just that. An event fast growing in popularity and enjoyed by runners of all abilities, this is one you really should think about doing if you fancy a day out by the seaside.

Where? Marine Parade, Brighton, East Sussex BN2 1TL

When? November

How many runners? Approximately 3,000

Why? A fun, fast and flat race, and a refreshing change from the hustle and bustle of big-city races.

5. Jane Tomlinson Leeds 10k

www.runforall.com

A new event for the North, but one that should be an inspiration to all those who followed the courageous

endeavours of the late Jane Tomlinson. This fast-growing event has developed a reputation for its friendly atmosphere and being a well-organised race.

Where? The Headrow, Leeds, West Yorkshire LS1

When? July

How many runners? Approximately 11,000

Why? New events can sometimes be a bit hit and miss, but all runners who have taken part in this one think it's an incredibly well-organised event with an atmosphere few other 10k races can rival – enough said!

❖fundraising for races

One of the reasons why the popularity of 5k and 10k running events have increased dramatically over the years is due to the number of races being organised by some of the UK's largest charities. The forever popular Race for Life events organised by Cancer Research UK for example, attract over half a million people every year to take part in a 5k or 10k race, with the sole purpose of encouraging participants to raise sponsorship money for their efforts.

Whatever event you choose to run in, be it a Race for Life 5k with thousands of participants, or a small 10k race in rural Gloucestershire, why not make your efforts that much more worthwhile and raise some money for a charity in the process? You needn't feel pressured to raise thousands of pounds (although that would be nice) but gentle encouragement of friends and family to sponsor you a few pounds here and there can make a big difference to local charities.

Fundraising tips

There are dozens of ways you can go about fundraising and encourage even your most miserly of friends to part with their cash for a good cause, so here are just a few to think about.

Target a time

If you have a competitive nature and are keen to walk or run your 5k or 10k under a certain time, why not suggest to friends, family and colleagues that if you cross the finish line under a certain time, they'll double their pledge? It's up to you how realistic you make the challenge, but tempting friends to have a bit of a flutter on whether you'll reach your goal can make the event that much more interesting.

Create a Just Giving page

The wonders of the internet have made it so much easier for people to make pledges online, negating the need for people to take themselves down to the cash point to withdraw some money to give to you once you've finished the race.

The website www.justgiving.co.uk is designed for people exactly like you who are training for an event and need to raise some sponsorship money. By creating a Just Giving page, you can state all the reasons you are training and why friends should make a donation to your chosen charity. By signing up with Just Giving, it makes life so much easier for everyone involved and it's so easy to keep track of how much money people are donating.

Host a party

Throwing a party to raise money is always a winner and without doubt the most fun way to raise money for your charity.

There are several ways to go about it, but making an occasion of a high profile sporting event such as The Grand National, FA Cup Final, Wimbledon or a 20/20 cricket match, is a great way to encourage people to come round to your house and watch the event together.

Once you have a dozen or so people, you can then raise money by having people pay a fee to place a bet on the final score, the winning horse, the goal scorer etc. Of course, the winner will get a token prize of £5 or a bottle of (cheap) sparkly, but the fun of a big get-together makes the occasion well worthwhile and an easy way to raise money. Be inventive and you'll be amazed at how easy it is to squeeze money out of people for a worthwhile cause.

useful websites

:running shoes/ clothes

With so many brands to choose from, it can be a nightmare knowing which brands are reputable and which are not. The following list includes the websites of some of the leading running kit companies.

www.adidas.com/uk

www.asics.co.uk

www.brooksrunning.co.uk

www.hellyhansen.com

www.mizuno.eu/gb-eng

www.newbalance.co.uk

www.newtonrunning.com

www.nikerunning.com

www.reebok.com

www.ronhill.com

www.salomon.com/uk

www.saucony.co.uk

www.shockabsorber.co.uk

:running gadgets

www.heartratemonitor.co.uk
One of the UK's leading suppliers of heart rate monitors and running gadgets, this is a must-visit website if you are interested in buying any technical running accessory.

www.polar.fi
Arguably the leading manufacturer of heart rate monitoring equipment, Polar produces both budget and advanced heart rate equipment.

www.garmin.co.uk
Garmin manufactures heart rate monitoring equipment and GPS watches to help runners navigate their training runs. Well worth the money if you like gadgets.

www.suunto.com
Suunto manufactures a range of great-looking, high-quality heart rate monitors. They might not be the cheapest on the market but they are certainly extremely well made and worth the investment.

www.timex.co.uk
Less popular than Polar but equally good, Timex manufactures great heart rate monitoring and timing products. Perfect for those interval training sessions.

:running magazines

Although the internet is by far the most popular medium for seeking out training advice, good old-fashioned magazines are still incredibly popular with the running community. The following publications in particular are full of great tips and worth considering subscribing to.

www.womensrunninguk.co.uk

A new publication launched in 2009, *Women's Running* covers a range of running topics applicable to both men and women. Excellent content and interesting features.

www.runnersworld.com

A favourite with many new and old runners, *Runner's World* produces quality articles every month, covering everything from injuries to nutrition.

www.runningfitnessmag.co.uk

Like *Runner's World*, *Running fitness* is a very good publication covering all running topics and is well worth a read.

www.runningfreemag.co.uk

Running free is free magazine distributed in leading running stores such as Runners Need, Up and Running and Run and Become. Great content and free to boot – a very worthwhile magazine for runners of all abilities.

:running resources

At some point during your training, you're likely to find yourself with an injury or training question, and you can bet that Google will be able to point you towards the answer. To save you time, the following websites contain a wealth of advice on all running topics and they are all worth bookmarking.

www.fitFAQS.co.uk

Packed full of general running and fitness tips, it also explodes plenty of common health and diet myths. Free training downloads on the running pages are used by dozens of UK charities, so it's well worth checking out.

www.runnersworld.co.uk

An invaluable resource for runners, giving plenty of information on training, injury prevention and upcoming races. The forum is always very active and a useful place to offload worries about training.

www.therunningbug.com

Forums, articles and reviews, the Running Bug is well worth bookmarking.

www.runningdiary.com

Lists all the major running events being held around the country, so well worth visiting to find 5k and 10k events in your area.

www.realbuzz.com

A general site for picking up fitness and running tips.

www.womensrunningnetwork.co.uk

An all-women's running movement founded in 1998 to inspire women of all ages to run for fun and fitness. It gives all women, whatever their age, size or ability, the opportunity to run together to improve their health, fitness, confidence and safety.

www.running4women.com

Product reviews, good races to run and an active forum to ask all the questions you have about training … running4women has it all.

www.runningforfun.co.uk

A simple site to navigate that is full of useful running tips.

www.mapmyrun.com

MapMyRun is an ingenious website that allows you to use satellite technology to show everyone your favourite running route – and run the favourite routes of fellow runners.

www.coolrunning.com

A great site for running tips and pace calculators.

www.jeffgalloway.com

Jeff Galloway is from the US and is a leading authority on running. His website will help answer most of your running questions.

www.runningforfitness.org

May be a little on the scientific side for some runners, this site will help to give you an idea of how to pace yourself for your training and the race itself.

www.runnersweb.co.uk

Here you'll find information on local running clubs, upcoming races and training. This is not an extensive site, but is still worth a visit.

www.physioroom.com

A one-stop shop for those niggling injuries, PhysioRoom has everything you need to treat an injury and get you back on the road.

www.runnersrescue.com

A concise site that will help you diagnose common injuries, offering sound advice on how to fix them.

online shopping

If you do most of your shopping online, then the following websites are those that you should consider visiting. However, never purchase your running shoes online unless you have had your running gait analysed and you know which make and size of running shoes are suitable for your gait. Buying them 'blind' can be a costly error in terms of the good of your training regime, so get assessed first and then go shopping on the virtual high street.

It's worth noting that the sites marked with an asterisk (*) also have high-street stores where you can have your running gait analysed; the website will help you to locate your nearest store.

www.girlsruntoo.co.uk

www.johnlewis.com

www.runnersneed.co.uk*

www.runningbath.co.uk*

www.simplyrun.co.uk*

www.sweatshop.co.uk*

www.sweatybetty.com

www.upandrunning.co.uk*

www.wiggle.co.uk

index